SAN DIEGO PUBLIC LIBRARY

LIBRARY RULES

TIME: — Books may be kept 14 days, unless dated otherwise.

RENEWALS: — Books may be renewed once at the agency where borrowed, unless on reserve. Bring book with you.

FINES: — Five cents a day will be charged for each book kept overtime.

DAMAGES: — *Injury to the book from tearing, penciling, unusual soiling or other ill-usage, will be charged to the card owner. Please report to us when a mutilated book is issued to you.*

CARDS—ALWAYS BRING YOUR CARD WITH YOU.

THE MOUNTAINS

O the Maountains, the Maountains,
They styarve a man, they styarve a man.
They grin, like sin,
They pin you in,
Till you go out and kyarve a man.

DORIS HALMAN
The 47 Varieties (1922)

THE MOUNTAINS

A PLAY IN ONE ACT

THE MOUNTAINS

A DRAMA IN THREE ACTS
AND A PROLOGUE

---

by THOMAS WOLFE

EDITED WITH AN INTRODUCTION *by Pat M. Ryan*

THE UNIVERSITY OF NORTH CAROLINA PRESS
CHAPEL HILL

To NORMAN HOLMES PEARSON,
mentor and friend.

ACKNOWLEDGMENTS

My thanks are due to Yale University Library for granting me extended use of the one-act script of *The Mountains;* to Harvard College Library for permitting me to examine and publish materials in the Thomas Wolfe Collection of William E. Wisdom (including the full-length version of *The Mountains*); to Richard S. Kennedy; and to The University of North Carolina Press, and Paul Gitlin, Administrator of the Thomas Wolfe Estate, for many kindnesses over several years. I am also indebted to Louise Sample, Reference Librarian of the Indiana-Purdue Regional Campus Library, Fort Wayne; Darrell Lemke, Reference Librarian of Indiana University Regional Campus Libraries; and Marilyn Strong, Interlibrary Loan Librarian of State University of New York, College at Brockport, for assistance in obtaining necessary books, articles, and ephemera.

For unfailing encouragement and patient prodding since 1958 (when I unearthed the one-act prompt script among George Pierce Baker papers at Yale), I wish to express my gratitude to my wife Jamice.

CONTENTS

ACKNOWLEDGMENTS / vii

THE TEXTS / xi

INTRODUCTION / 3
BIBLIOGRAPHY / 47

The Mountains:
A PLAY IN ONE ACT BY THOMAS WOLFE / 53

The Mountains:
A DRAMA IN THREE ACTS AND
A PROLOGUE BY THOMAS WOLFE / 87

THE TEXTS

I have so edited the one-act version of *The Mountains* as to reflect both Wolfe's "final" script (41 pages) and the circumstances of its production (deletions, additions, stage directions). The author's stage directions, thus, appear uniformly in parentheses (as Wolfe wrote them), while the director's and stage manager's notes are given in brackets. I have generally followed the original punctuation and spelling; and I have retained the script's inconsistent nature of stage directions—alternately abbreviated and spelled out (e.g., "R." for right, "L." for left, "C." for center). I have silently emended "L." (for Laura) to "Laura" and "R." (for Richard) to "Richard," however; and I have altered "Dick" to "Richard" in a couple of stage directions. I have also emended each directorial "x" (for cross) to "cross(es)." Intermittent footnotes will indicate the extent and nature of revision in production—relatively slight.

The full-length version ("A Drama in Three Acts and a Prologue") is here printed for the first time in substantially the form Wolfe delivered to George Pierce Baker: a neat typescript of 159 pages (Prologue and Act I, 70 pages; Act II, 26 pages; Act III, 63 pages). I have emended "Gudge" to "Gudger" in two places in the Prologue, deleted Wolfe's second-act dramatis personae, and supplied a complete list of characters at the head of the text. Otherwise, the manuscript (except for the omission of Baker's marginal comments) is published essentially as Wolfe left it, in 1922.

INTRODUCTION

INTRODUCTION

"It is only fair to tell you that my interests are centered in the drama, and that someday I hope to write successfully for the theatre and to do nothing but that." When Thomas Wolfe in January, 1924, applied for a position teaching English at New York University, he confessed to "no experience" as a teacher and emphasized that a play of his, written while a Harvard graduate student, was then in the hands of a New York producer. But "even in the fortunate event of its acceptance," he acquiesced, "I feel the necessity of finding immediate employment."[1]

Wolfe got the job, but did not sell his script (*Welcome to Our City*) to the Theatre Guild—or to any other producer. And though D. Appleton & Company editors later expressed interest in reading the play, Wolfe declined to submit this work for book publication.

His tormented drive to become a professional playwright was blunted neither by refusal of his script nor by the exhausting pace of NYU teaching duties. During a four-day Easter respite from theme grading, Wolfe managed to complete "almost an entire act" of a new play; and, during a ten-day May final examination period, and intermittently through the summer, he again wrestled with this script—the germ of *Mannerhouse*.

The following December (1925), in Paris, when a bag containing two acts and a prologue of this play was stolen from his hotel, Wolfe wrote Homer A. Watt that "nothing has hit me like this since the death of my brother Ben." He moved to another hotel, bought some paper, and within a fortnight had "not only recreated what was lost, but completed an entire first draft."[2] In the fall and winter of 1925–26, Wolfe offered *Mannerhouse* and a revised *Welcome to Our City* to the Theatre Guild, the Provincetown Players, and the Neighborhood Playhouse. But he sold neither play.

The would-be playwright's course of frustration terminated with the New York commercial stage's unremitting rejection of his scripts in 1924, 1925, and 1926. Teaching at NYU continued part-

1. *The Correspondence of Thomas Wolfe and Homer Andrew Watt*, eds. Oscar Cargill and Thomas Clark Pollock (New York, 1954), p. 3.
2. *Ibid.*, p. 10.

time and full-time until 1930; and only with reluctance did Wolfe ultimately turn from drama and to the writing of fiction, and produce his first novel, *Look Homeward, Angel,* issued by Scribner's in 1929.

"It took Wolfe three and a half long years to realize that he had not been born to be a dramatist," biographer Elizabeth Nowell wrote, "and five years more before he emerged as a full-fledged novelist."[3] Yet his dramatic apprenticeship—first with The Carolina Playmakers, then in Harvard 47 Workshop, and finally on the New York commercial theatre scene—was the crucible in which his art as a writer of fiction was both formed and refined.

CAROLINA PLAYMAKING

Thomas Clayton Wolfe was born October 3, 1900, the youngest of William Oliver and Julia Elizabeth (Westall) Wolfe's eight children, at 92 Woodfin Street, in Asheville, North Carolina. He grew up in the mountain town of his birth; entered Orange Street Public School in 1905; and moved, with his mother and brother Ben, to the large home on Spruce Street which Mrs. Wolfe operated as a boardinghouse, in 1906. He attended North State School, a boys' private college preparatory school conducted by Mr. and Mrs. J. M. Roberts, from 1912 (the year of its founding) until 1916, when he entered The University of North Carolina at Chapel Hill.

It is a durable Asheville legend (fostered by *Look Homeward, Angel*) that Wolfe in his boyhood "read everything, good and bad, that the town library contained"; and Margaret Roberts, his first literary mentor, is supposed to have declared (before taking him as her student), on first reading some of his classroom writing: "Well, he is a genius!" Just before graduating from North State School, Tom Wolfe won first place and a bronze medal for his essay "Shakespeare the Man," written for a contest sponsored by the *Independent Magazine.* Eugene Gant's adolescent torments in

---

3. Elizabeth Nowell, *Thomas Wolfe: A Biography* (New York, 1960), p. 50. Clifford Odets, meeting Wolfe for the first time in 1935, discovered that he was "very stagestruck" and "said that he had always wanted to be a playwright, not a novelist" (Drama Section, *New York Times,* September 14, 1958, p. 3).

the "My Shakespeare, rise!" incident of *Look Homeward, Angel* of course derive from this proud moment of its author's youth: the actual 1916 prize essay ends with Ben Jonson's affectionate exhortation "My Shakespeare, rise!"

In a typed page deleted from *O Lost!* (the huge manuscript which, reshaped, became *Look Homeward, Angel*), Wolfe also recalled that one of the buildings lining Asheville's Church Street was a theatre: "Recessed cunningly behind and above Miller and Brown's shoestore is the Grand Opera House, centre of the city's nocturnal and recreational festivity. Here comes every year for its grand opening the celebrated Al G. Fields minstrel troupe, Honeyboy Evans, and the cream of New York's musical and dramatic attractions."[4] But neither his ensuing list of plays performed there (titles nostalgically recalling the turn-of-century Anglo-American stage) nor the Whitmanesque catalogue of books read by young Tom-Eugene suggests that in his boyhood Wolfe was perceptibly stage-struck.

He did not experience strongly the lure of the theatre until his third year at Chapel Hill, when Professor Frederick H. Koch, late of George Pierce Baker's Harvard 47 Workshop and the Dakota Playmakers, came to The University of North Carolina and founded The Carolina Playmakers.

Wolfe's rambling autobiographical notebooks, jotted down preliminary to the writing of *O Lost!* reveal that during the junior year at The University of North Carolina ". . . my gregariousness reached its highest peak. I joined everything." Concerning Pro-

4. Harvard College Library MS *46AM-7(26). Wolfe's selection of detail here is significant. The minstrel show had been a pivotal element in *Welcome to Our City* (1923); whereas, by the time of Wolfe's boyhood, this tradition had dwindled to insignificance in historical Asheville. Cf. typescript of A. L. S., Wolfe to Frederick H. Koch, New York, Saturday night, May [3?] 1924, Harvard College Library: "I knew nothing of the theatre at that time [1919–20]. Possibly I had seen a half dozen plays in all my life"; Donald J. Rulfs, "The Theater in Asheville from 1879 to 1931," *North Carolina Historical Review*, XXXVI (October, 1959), 429–41. In *Look Homeward, Angel* (New York, 1929), p. 153, Eugene Gant, in autumn, 1907, makes a two-week trip with his father to Augusta, Georgia, where they see a play together: "They went to the theatre: it was one of the first plays he had seen. The play was a biblical one, founded on the story of Saul and Jonathan, and he had whispered to Gant from scene to scene the trend of coming events—a precocity which pleased his father mightily, and to which he referred for months."

fessor Koch and The Playmakers, though, he was retrospectively disenchanted: "The character of Koch—man with one obsession. One Idea that would not hold water—Fanatical zeal—The ethical-practical. Would convince himself that any labor he was engaged—of whatever sort—was sanctified. . . . Execrable play well spoken of. . . . The folk drama and other cant. Everyone was very grim—Youth has not the zest and skill for comedy."[5]

In an unpublished playwriting-apprenticeship section of *O Lost!* moreover, Wolfe translated these misgivings into seven savage and sardonic, but insightful, pages. Koch is here cruelly lampooned as Professor Hutch, "the Little Man with the Urge," for whom an ingenuous Eugene dutifully composed folk-plays: "He wrote plays. They were one act long. He wrote, since he was hillborn, of mountaineers. He knew little of them. He knew about people in boardinghouses and small towns. But he wrote about mountaineers who went bang-bang. The teacher who taught playwriting called them folk-plays. A folk-play is a play in which people say 'Hit ain't' and 'that air.' Eugene wrote about mountaineers who went bang-bang. Some of the students wrote about tenant farmers and fishermen. One or two wrote about 'the problem of the Negro.' "[6]

The deleted section on folk-plays in *O Lost!* is quite as brutal in its parody of Wolfe's early one-acter, *The Return of Buck Gavin*:

> He wrote his plays during a single afternoon, in the cold grey rains of autumn. One was about an outlaw mountaineer who returned to put violets on the grave of a comrade killed in a battle with the revenooers. He called it The Return of Jed Sevier. It was a folk-play. . . .
>
> JED (*wearily*): Let 'em come. Whut do I keer now that Jim's gone? (*The door opens slowly. The Sheriff stands covering Jed with a six-shooter.*)
> MARY (*with a cry*): Jed!

5. Harvard College Library MS *46AM–7(25).
6. Harvard College Library MS *46AM–7(26). Koch himself unwittingly delivered as telling an indictment of folk-plays in "The Drama in the South," *Carolina Play-Book*, XIII, ii (June, 1940), 61. Here, he recalls having discouraged a Chinese student from writing a play about "the Chinese-American problem—a mixed marriage of a Chinese boy and an American girl," as follows: " 'A good idea, but you can't do it.—We should like to have you write of your own people. You have a marvelous store of legend in old China. We are interested in what we call the "folk play." I wish you would write for us a Chinese folk play.' "

THE SHERIFF (*slowly*): I reckon I've got ye this time, Jed.
JED (*wheels as if shot with his hand to his hip. Then slowly
he raises his hands in a gesture of surrender. Quietly*): Hit's the law.
Ye cain't buck it! Hit'll get ye in the end.

(*CURTAIN*)

This was a folk-play.

And, further on, he takes what is clearly a self-critical swipe at
The Mountains, a script of his begun at Chapel Hill and completed
and performed at Harvard:

DICK (*he is a sensitive intelligent-looking boy of 15, but already bent and worn by hard work and hunger*): Paw, Perfessor
Jenkins said I cain't come back to school no more 'less I git some
books.

JIM (*with a sudden outburst of blind rage, slapping the boy
across the mouth*): I ain't got no money to waste on books, ye little
bastard.

(*There is a pause.*)

SAL (*slowly*): I reckon them things ain't fer the like o' us.
... Whut's it all about Jim?
JIM (*wearily*): God knows.

(*CURTAIN*)

This was "a tragedy of the soil." The business was fantastic enough to
the young men, who were really creating crude romantic fiction of a
life they knew little about. Most of them were dwellers in quiet streets,
the sons of merchants, lawyers, doctors. But they never wrote about
these people. A folk-play was not about the folks one knew.
But to the Little Man with the Urge it was Truth, Beauty, Reality.
... The renascence of society, the cultivation of the masses, the future
of mankind all depended on folk-plays. What a Folk-Play was he did
not know very clearly. It was a communal emanation, Eugene gathered,
of thousands of people, mysteriously transferred to paper by a single
elect spokesman. . . .
Through this strange man, Eugene first saw the bright false world of
the theatre. He learned the slogans, talked the jargon, believed the cant.
It was years before he came to the more sophisticated twaddle—"tempo,"
"pace," "boldly stylized conventions," "staccato cadences," stage set-

tings, lights, expressionism, and the rest of it, but, steeped in the music of immortal poetry, he began to read the not too modern classics of the footlights—Ibsen, Shaw, Barrie, Lady Gregory, Dunsany, O'Neill, and to swallow down all that was told him with pious obedience. His instinct told him that, compared with the work of the great men in modern literature, most of this was at best poor stuff, and that the first-rate artist in modern life, with his desperate need for plastic loneliness, will not pool his dark soul in with the vanities of twittering women and the gabbling half-men.

But he had been touched by the lights of carnival, and all beyond those lights was phantom—the smell of the paint, the witch magic of the lights, the transforming glow of wonder, which lends enchantment to all the old banalities, and which is really the unique and enchanting thing about it all. Little could be said—little that had wonder for fine and subtle consciences—but with what glory and magnificence! Eugene —like the Little Man with the Urge—was bewitched; he believed it all.

The embittered author of these lines had been chastened by nearly a decade of fruitless striving for acceptance as a dramatist. College classmates had mocked his earnest attempts and Broadway producers had spurned them. The wonder of it is that Tom Wolfe did not in the end abandon writing altogether.

During the Chapel Hill years (1916–20), however, it was not playmaking Professor Koch, but English Professor Edwin Greenlaw, archetype for Randolph Ware in *The Web and the Rock*, who most crucially directed Wolfe toward his eventual self-anatomizing style. Wolfe had met Greenlaw in his sophomore year, in an English literature survey which thoroughly inoculated him with Greenlaw's theory of literature as a "transcript of life" (to be articulated in his book *The Province of Literary History*).[7] He took Greenlaw's Elizabethan drama course in his junior year and Greenlaw's nondramatic Renaissance literature and advanced composi-

---

7. "Such a history takes into account literature as reflecting not the externals of contemporary manners alone, but the spiritual conflicts of an age; an epoch is rarely to be explained in terms of a single proposition, since its life is very complex and filled with cross currents; and finally, the 'life' of an age or of a representative major intellect of that age is not a matter of household economy, daily experience, party warfare, but includes the intellectual sources, the influence of a past time, transformed or translated in terms of the age or of the writer's genius," Edwin Greenlaw, *The Province of Literary History* (Baltimore, 1931), pp. 84–85. Cf. James Holly Hanford, "Edwin Greenlaw and the Study of Literature," *Studies in Philology*, XXIX (April, 1932), 141–48.

tion courses in his senior year. Elizabeth Nowell has proposed that the "thorough soaking" he got in Elizabethan literature was of paramount importance: "As some of Wolfe's more discerning critics pointed out years later, he was in many ways an Elizabethan, and that quality is one of the richest and most enduring in his work."[8]
The genesis for one of Wolfe's earliest attempts at dramatic writing, a one-act script entitled *The Strikers*, was a group writing project in Greenlaw's advanced composition class. After reading John Galsworthy's drama *Strife* to this class, Wolfe recalled, Greenlaw launched his students upon the collective composition of a novel about a strike: "My part, the breaking of the strike and the two men on the verandah high above town, Greenlaw said I had achieved 'style'—which most men don't get till forty. The *creative instinct* and the ebullience of the good in me. . . ."[9]
(And just following this reminiscence, Wolfe exults: "Is not this the true romantic feeling—not to desire to escape life, but to prevent life from escaping you?—Imperfect apprehension, yet these things which are good are so magnificently good—and usually so easy of acquisition—that perhaps the rest is only the opening of doors as yet unfound"—lines which anticipate Wolfe's symbolic prose poem prefacing *Look Homeward, Angel*, " . . . a stone, a leaf, an unfound door. . . ."[10])
It was also Greenlaw who, as head of the English Department at Chapel Hill, had first promoted the creation of The Carolina Playmakers; his imagination and loyalty, according to Koch, "made possible the remarkable growth of a native folk drama here."[11] Later, at Harvard, Wolfe began, but left uncompleted, a play based on the opposing philosophies of the two teachers he regarded as most influential in his life: Greenlaw, the scientific and "thoroughgoing teutonized scholar,"[12] and Horace Williams, the idealistic

8. *Thomas Wolfe: A Biography*, p. 40.
9. Harvard College Library MS *46AM-7(25).
10. Cf. E. K. Brown, "Thomas Wolfe: Realist and Symbolist," *University of Toronto Quarterly*, X (January, 1941), 219.
11. Frederick H. Koch (ed.), *Carolina Folk Plays* (New York, 1922), p. xvi.
12. ["Professor Weldon"] Harvard College Library MS *46AM-7(21): "Professor X is a strong, active man in the very prime of his life. He is a tireless worker and rarely gets to bed before three in the morning. His hero is Sir Francis Bacon and his slogan is method."

obscurantist, Hegelian-Unitarian whose ideas profoundly affected his ethical outlook (and whom he dubbed the "Hegel of the cotton-patch").[13] This fragment ("The Old School"), reshaped, became part of Act One of his full-length *The Mountains*, and Williams also provided the model for Colonel Tasker Weldon in *Mannerhouse* and for Virgil Weldon in *Look Homeward, Angel*.

The tangible product of Wolfe's two years in Professor Koch's playwriting class is meager, at best. In an exuberant essay on "Folk-Play Making," introducing his *Carolina Folk Plays* anthology, Koch had claimed: "The stories and characters are drawn by the writers from their own tradition, and from the observation of the lives of their own people. They are wholly native—simple plays of the locality, of common experience and of common interest."[14] Yet *The Return of Buck Gavin*, a "regional" hill-country play included on The Carolina Playmakers' first program, March 14 and 15, 1919, was thrown together at the eleventh hour, the night before Wolfe's script was due. (Paul Green, also a charter member of the group, has attested that this tendency was chronic with his classmate, who would turn up in class ostentatiously unkempt after these all-night's agonies to read the rarely impressive result to his fellows.)[15] The "rural" character of Buck Gavin (whom Wolfe himself portrayed in the play's two performances, directed by Greek professor W. S. Bernard) was in fact modeled after real-life, urban Patrick "Cyclone Pat" Lavein, a Texas gangster whose capture in Chicago was reported in the *Grand Forks* (N.D.) *Her-*

13. Williams' lectures for 1921–22 were published posthumously as *Logic for Living*, ed. Jane Ross Hammer (New York, 1951). In the incomplete "Professor Weldon" script, Wolfe wrote: "The first day I attended the Logic under Mr. W. he said: 'Gentlemen, there's no such thing as a fact.'" Cf. Henry Horace Williams, *The Evolution of Logic* (Chapel Hill, 1925) and *The Education of Horace Williams* (Chapel Hill, 1936); Robert Winston, *Horace Williams, Gadfly of Chapel Hill* (Chapel Hill, 1942).

14. *Carolina Folk Plays*, p. xi. Cf. Koch, "Teaching Playwriting," *The Carolina Play-book*, II, i (March, 1929), 33: "Playwriting cannot be taught in the conventional way. The use of a textbook tends to make the young writer self-conscious. It is likely to inhibit his impulse, to limit his imagination, to mar his design. He must look about him and let his materials determine his design."

15. Recounted by James K. Hutsell, "As They Recall Thomas Wolfe," *Southern Packet*, IV (April, 1948), 4.

ald, where Wolfe happened upon it; and tradition has it that Wolfe dashed off this script in three hours flat.[16]

"When the dramatic possibilities of the incident flashed upon me," Wolfe records in his foreword to the play, "I immediately started to work with a set of mountain characters." (Soon afterward, he would write in *O Lost!*: "He knew about people in boardinghouses and small towns. But he wrote about mountaineers. . . .") He then pleads compellingly, if academically, the case for an apprentice writer's turning to the near and known, rather than to the romantic and remote: "But the dramatic is not the unusual. It is happening daily in our lives. Some of us, perhaps, toil on a mountain farm, and when we relax from the stolidity of mind and allow ourselves thought, it is to think bitterly on the unvaried, monotonous grind of our existence. Here is drama in the true sense."[17] Yet his own script, notwithstanding its contemporary, Carolina mountains setting, mainly traffics in melodrama and sentiment. More a vignette than a play (comprising barely twelve printed pages), *The Return of Buck Gavin* relates how the fugitive protagonist is prevented from laying flowers at his bootlegger brother's grave on "the top o' the Smoky" by the arrival of the sheriff. At final curtain, Buck lays the violets and arbutus in his sister Mary's lap: "Well, I reckon I cain't go now . . . but ol' Jim'll know . . . jes' the same. Sis,—you take 'em."

A second play, the brief *Deferred Payment* (not performed), was published in the June, 1919, number of *The Magazine*. A third, *The Third Night*,[18] "A Ghost Play of the Carolina Mountains," produced December 12 and 13, 1919, is briefer and less deserving of notice than *Buck Gavin*.[19] Playmaker Koch's sanction of plays

16. Cf. Wolfe, "Writing Is My Life," *The Atlantic Monthly*, CLXXVIII (December, 1946), 64: "I wrote it on a rainy night, when I was seventeen, in three hours" [letter to Mrs. J. M. Roberts, New York, May 5, 1924]; typescript of A. L. S., Wolfe to Frederick H. Koch, Saturday night, May [3?] 1924, Harvard College Library: "I wrote that play at one sitting, on a rainy October afternoon, when I was seventeen or eighteen."

17. Frederick H. Koch (ed.), *Carolina Folk Plays, Second Series* (New York, 1924), p. 115.

18. Published in Frederick H. Koch (ed.), *Carolina Folk Plays, First, Second, and Third Series* (New York, 1941), pp. 70–75.

19. Claude William LaSalle II is the first Wolfe scholar to have paid critical attention to the early one-act scripts, "Thomas Wolfe: The Dramatic

based on "North Carolina folk-superstitution,"[20] however, had partly deflected Wolfe from writing about "the unvaried, monotonous grind of our existence." Like its predecessors, *The Third Night* was "a play in which people say 'Hit ain't' and 'that air.' " A fourth play, the topical comedy *Concerning Honest Bob*, was published in the May, 1920, number of *The Magazine*.[21]

Richard S. Kennedy, though generally endorsing Wolfe's demurrers regarding Koch and his methods, pleads "two important results" in extenuation: "First, he was introduced to a writing method that he later used in his significant work. Frederick Koch (who had adopted the idea from [George Pierce] Baker, urged all his students to use the materials of their own experience in their writing. . . . [Second,] it is one of the fortunate ironies of Thomas Wolfe's life that [Koch's] undiscriminating encouragement launched him on a writing career that was to become the center of his existence for the rest of his life."[22] And Wolfe himself, in a mild, compliant "Biographical Statement" written as a final assignment for Koch's playwriting class, had forecast better than he knew: "If they [the folk plays] have . . . indirectly caused an analysis of my writing and a determination of my future course,— are they not worthwhile, even though they be but the amateurish productions of a youngster, at the best?"[23]

Wolfe's most prolific writing at Chapel Hill actually had been campus journalism, not drama. He was a regular contributor to the *Tar Baby*, the college humor magazine; was the wartime mainstay of the *Tar Heel*, as reporter, feature writer, and, during his junior and senior years, editor; and was associate editor-in-chief of *The Magazine*, in whose pages his earliest poetry and short fiction

Apprenticeship" (Ph.D. thesis, University of Pennsylvania, 1964). Paschal Reeves's edition of Wolfe's one-act plays (University of Georgia Press) is imminent.

20. Koch (ed.), *Carolina Folk Plays* (1941), p. xvii.

21. A satiric "melodrama," *The Streets of Durham; or, Dirty Work at the Crossroads: A Tragedy in Three Muddy Acts*, was included in Wolfe's marathon tour de force, the April 20, 1920, issue of *Tar Baby* (whose entire 44 pages he wrote alone, in one night).

22. Richard S. Kennedy, *The Window of Memory: The Literary Career of Thomas Wolfe* (Chapel Hill, 1962), pp. 48–49.

23. "Tom Wolfe on the Drama," ed. Frank Kearns, *Carolina Quarterly*, XI (1960), 10.

appeared—including "A Cullenden of Virginia," his first short story.[24]

"The desire to write, which had been strong during all my days in high school, grew stronger still," Wolfe recalled fifteen years later. "I was . . . still thinking I would become a lawyer or a newspaperman, never daring to believe I could seriously become a writer."[25] Accordingly, in his application to the Harvard Graduate School, he wrote: "In considering this application you should know that I have decided on Journalism as my work."[26]

HARVARD 47 WORKSHOP

Wolfe's three years of graduate study at Harvard University were easily as tumultuous as his fictionalized treatment of them in *Of Time and the River*. He reached Cambridge in late September, 1920, established cramped living quarters in an attic room of a house rented by a Chapel Hill professor and his family, and almost at once sought out George Pierce Baker.

"How I became a 47'er," he jotted in his notebook. "Met G. P. first time going to his office—The thin lips—the broad hat—perhaps his conception of the artist type—I get in."[27] One morning, without ceremony, Wolfe presented himself at the door of Professor Baker's residence and, after being ushered by Mrs. Baker into her famous husband's study, told Baker he wanted to enroll in English 47,

24. "I also remember a short story—my first—which was called 'A Winchester of Virginia,' and was about the recreant son of an old family, who recovered his courage and vindicated his tarnished honor in the charge over the top that took his life," Wolfe, *You Can't Go Home Again* (New York, 1940), p. 711. The 1920 *Yackety Yack*, University of North Carolina yearbook, lists Wolfe's student activities as follows [numbers 2, 3, and 4 designate sophomore, junior, and senior years]: "Di Society; Buncombe County Club; Freshman-Sophomore debate (2); Dramatic Association; Carolina Playmakers (3, 4), author of two one-act plays; Executive Committee (4); Associate Editor *Yackety Yack* (3); Associate Editor [*Carolina*] *Magazine* (3), Assistant Editor-in-Chief (4); Advisory Board *Tar Baby* (4); Worth Prize in Philosophy (3); Y.M.C.A. Cabinet (3, 4); Student Council (4); Class Poet (3, 4); Chairman Junior Stunt Committee; German Club; Amphoterothen; Satyrs; Golden Fleece; Sigma Epsilon; Omega Delta; Pi Kappa Phi."
25. *The Story of a Novel* (New York, 1949), p. 5.
26. Harvard University Archives, UAV 101.201.10. Registrar's Office folder for Thomas Wolfe.
27. Harvard College Library MS *46AM–7(25).

the select "Baker's Dozen," better known as 47 Workshop. Notwithstanding Wolfe's Carolina Playmaker credentials, Baker at first declined. But Wolfe telegraphed a distressed appeal to Koch; Koch mailed back *The Return of Buck Gavin* and *The Third Night;* and Wolfe, at length, was invited to join "the sacred circle."

He also enrolled that first year in Baker's drama survey, in Chester Greenough's American literature class, and in John Livingston Lowes's course on the English Romantic poets, and audited George Lyman Kittredge's Shakespeare class (Wolfe's notebooks contain generous allusions to " 'Johnny' Lowes and the Romantic poets" and to "that noble scholar 'Kitty' ").[28] Baker's English 47 playwriting class, of course, was for three years the center of his Cambridge universe. The Workshop (as he later expressed it in *Of Time and the River*) was

... the rock to which his life was anchored, the rudder of his destiny, the sole and all-sufficient reason for his being here. It now seemed to him that there was only one work in life which he could possibly do, and that this work was writing plays, and that if he could not succeed in this work he had better die, since any other life than the life of the playwright and the theatre was not to be endured. Accordingly every interest and energy of his life was now fastened on this work with a madman's passion; he thought, felt, breathed, ate, drank, slept and lived completely in terms of plays.[29]

Baker had inaugurated course-work in dramatic theory and playwriting at Radcliffe College in 1903, and at Harvard in 1905; he launched the Workshop, under that name—dedicated to the writing and production of plays—in 1912–13. By the time of Wolfe's advent in Cambridge, Baker's illustrious English 47 students included playwrights Edward Sheldon, S. N. Behrman, Philip Barry, Sidney Howard, and Eugene O'Neill; drama writers and critics Leslie Hotson, Kenneth Macgowan, Ward Morehouse, Heywood Broun, Robert Benchley, and John Mason Brown; theatrical de-

28. *Ibid.* Cf. Wolfe letter to Edwin Greenlaw, Cambridge, spring, 1922: "Professor Lowes' book on Coleridge [*The Road to Xanadu*] had a great effect on me. In that book he shows conclusively how retentive of all it reads is the mind and how, at almost any moment, that mass of material may be fused and resurrected in new and magic forms." *The Letters of Thomas Wolfe,* ed. Elizabeth Nowell (New York, 1956), p. 30.

29. *Of Time and the River* (New York, 1935), p. 130.

signers Robert Edmond Jones, Lee Simonson, and Donald Oen-slager; Theatre Guild directors Theresa Helburn and Maurice Wertheim; drama professors Alan Reynolds Thompson, Stanley McCandless, and Frederick H. Koch; and many others. Ward Morehouse and Kenneth Raisbeck (the model for Francis Starwick in *Of Time and the River*) were Baker's teaching assistants while Wolfe was in the class; John Mason Brown and Dorothy Sands acted leading roles in public performances of Wolfe's *The Mountains;* and Donald Oenslager and Stanley McCandless supervised design and lighting phases of this October, 1922, Workshop one-acts bill.

Wolfe's initial impressions of the other, older 1920–21 Workshop members were less than cordial. "When [they] criticize," he confided in a letter to Koch, "it is as follows: 'Sir Arthur Pinero takes that scene and treats it with *consummate art*' or 'the remarkable literary charm of this play seduces my admiration.' Prof, so help me, God, these are direct quotations. Imagine a raw Tar Heel who with native simplicity has been accustomed to wade into a play (at Chapel Hill) with 'that's great stuff' or 'Rotten'—simple and concise."[30] And this first reaction, as Elizabeth Nowell has pointed out, "was his true and final reaction."[31] His retrospective notebook entries are quite as harsh: "The way the Workshop crowd could be swept away at the moment by a bad play, inherit the damnation of the audience, swiftly change over, and make mirth with it at the end of the year. Easy for second-rate people to burlesque bad writing—gain a reputation for cleverness by it. . . . That hatred which ungenerous and ambitious youth has for success—*Poor old* Barrie—Poor *old* Shaw—*Poor old* Galsworthy (who wrote some fair plays once—at first)—Contempt for the certain thing—on the spy for the tangled thing—From such as these are minor poets made."[32]

Philip Barber, a Workshop member during Wolfe's second year at Harvard, afterwards wrote that Wolfe himself regularly and freely indulged in "psychic cannibalism" during English 47 criticism sessions: "As Tom cut and carved and tore and pounded, the

---

30. Cambridge, November 26, 1920. *Letters of Thomas Wolfe*, p. 10.
31. Nowell, *Thomas Wolfe: A Biography*, p. 52.
32. Harvard College Library MS *46AM-7(25).

excitement grew, and vitality entered him."[33] Predictably, Wolfe's overt ill feelings were reciprocated. New York drama critic Ward Morehouse, for instance, recalled in 1950: "Oh, yes, I knew Wolfe, but I never liked him. I was introduced to him a couple of times, but whenever I saw him in the Yard, I cut him."[34] Miss Nowell, with simple eloquence, has put it frankly: "These young men and women at Harvard considered him as something of a freak."[35]

In *Of Time and the River* Wolfe cast his still smouldering resentments into narrative form, in the knot of Cambridge snobs he described as "people without talent and without sincerity of soul or integrity of purpose, [who] were given a formula for knowledge; a language that sounded very knowing, expert, and assured, and yet that knew nothing, was experienced in nothing, was sure of nothing."[36] In his May, 1938, Purdue speech, he went on to acknowledge that he himself had succumbed to this intellectual climate: "I am afraid . . . I talked a great deal more about 'beauty' and 'art' than I created it; expended a great deal more time in scorning and ridiculing 'the bourgeoisie' than in trying to find out who they were and what they were like."[37]

Even his first-year adulation of Baker, in time, dwindled into disillusion. In a section deleted from *Of Time and the River* Wolfe wrote (of "Professor Hatcher"): "I worshipped him for almost a year. He was the great man, the prophet, the infinitely wise and strong and gentle spirit who knew all, had seen all, could solve all problems by a word, release us of all the anguish, grief and error of our lives by a wave of his benevolent hand."[38] Reminiscences of "the great man" in his notebooks are less generous:

Baker—talked too much—Asked questions of other people revealing himself—Asked four people to keep confidential what he had already told six. . . . Baker's carefully insinuated letters from Eugene O'Neill. Baker's comparison—"First Dickens—then I discovered my Meredith. Well? It was pitiful how inadequate Dickens seemed." We were always

33. "Tom Wolfe Writes a Play," *Harper's*, CCXVI (May, 1958), 52.
34. Kennedy, *The Window of Memory*, p. 66.
35. Nowell, *Thomas Wolfe: A Biography*, p. 52.
36. *Of Time and the River*, p. 135.
37. *Thomas Wolfe's Purdue Speech "Writing and Living*," eds. William Braswell and Leslie A. Field (West Lafayette, Ind., 1964), p. 48.
38. Cited by Nowell, *Thomas Wolfe: A Biography*, p. 52.

getting a little beyond.—Baker, who never failed to mention Jones or Pinero—his friendships with them—when he could—was secretly afraid things would pass him by as it had them. . . . In spite of his vast assumption of worldliness—a naively ignorant man.[39]

It was under Baker's aegis, though, in an at times hostile Workshop, that Thomas Wolfe took his first giant steps forward as a writer. Even *The Mountains,* whose failure in performance caused him "almost inconceivable anguish and despair,"[40] in the end forced him to a greater self-discipline than he had ever known during the Chapel Hill years. "Koch's emphasis was continually on the content of the play, and his greatest influence was in directing Wolfe's choice of materials," as Claude W. LaSalle II has remarked. "Baker's emphasis was always on the technical devices necessary to the drama, and his great influence on Wolfe was in the area of techniques."[41]

The Mountains, originally in one-act form, then expanded to three acts and a prologue, constitutes its author's earliest achieved writing on a large, Wolfean scale. Begun while he was still in Chapel Hill, the one-act version was completed at Cambridge in time for a trial performance in the Workshop rehearsal room on January 25, 1921;[42] and, revised, *The Mountains,* A Drama in One Act, was put into rehearsal October 5 and produced at Agassiz House Theatre, Radcliffe, on October 21 and 22, 1921.[43]

39. Harvard College Library MS *46AM-7(25).
40. *Letters of Thomas Wolfe,* p. 428.
41. LaSalle, "Thomas Wolfe: The Dramatic Apprenticeship," p. 66. Cf. Andrew Turnbull, *Thomas Wolfe* (New York, 1968), p. 46: "Baker's enterprise *was* commercial, albeit in the best sense. With his belief in the theater as a civilizing force, he took pride in those of his students who went on to New York successes. . . ."
42. The trial performance, "produced by Mr. Williams," presented William F. Manley as Richard, Mr. Bond as Dr. Weaver, Miss Snyder as Laura, J. J. Daly as Tom Weaver, Mr. Rice as Roberts, and W. G. Thomas as Sam.
43. The October, 1921, production presented John Mason Brown as Dr. Weaver, William F. Manley as Richard, Dorothy Sands as Laura, J. J. Daly as Tom Weaver, Doris Halman as Mag Weaver, R. McConnell as Roberts, and W. G. Thomas as Sam. Each of these two performances was attended by an invited audience of three hundred persons (*Harvard Crimson,* October 22, 1921, p. 1).
The epigraph on p. ii is attributed by Richard S. Kennedy, "Thomas Wolfe at Harvard, 1920-1923," *Harvard Library Bulletin,* IV, ii (Spring,

"It is the real thing," he assured his mother, "and deals with a great tragedy, the tragedy of a fine young man who returns to his mountains with fine dreams and ideals of serving his people. It is not a feud play, altho the feud is used. The tragedy of the play is the tragedy of this fine young man fighting against conditions that overcome him and destroy him in the end. When you read this play I hope you will be aware of this tragedy and the tragedy of the lot of those poor oppressed mountain people, old and worn out at middle-age by their terrific hopeless battle with the mountain, . . . shutting these people eternally away from the world, hemming them in, guarding them, and finally killing them."[44]

A fortnight after the January rehearsal room tryout, he told his Asheville and Chapel Hill friend George V. Denny, Jr., that *The Mountains* would likely be given a full production: "The play is faulty in places at present, but these I can correct in my revision. It is an honest, true, and in places, powerful piece of work. This is the truth, so I see no reason why I should deny it. I'm by no means a shining or burning light in the dramatic firmament up here, but I have been told it is by all odds the best play written in the class this year."[45] And the following summer, confident of his completed revision, he sent a copy via his mother and Mrs. Margaret Roberts to Erville Alderson, of the Ridpath Chautauqua Company, offering it for possible touring production: "The actual story, the definite human story, in the foreground, the story of a young doctor who is finally done in by powerful and irresistible forces is not the only thing I'm trying to convey. In the background is the story of an entire race chained by the tyranny of the mountains which beat them down year by year."[46]

Wolfe's acute disappointment at the cool reception accorded *The Mountains* by Cambridge audiences[47] has been poignantly re-

---

1950), 189, to Doris Halman, who portrayed Mag and wrote lyrics for the 1922 Harvard revue *The 47 Varieties*.

44. *The Letters of Thomas Wolfe to His Mother*, eds. C. Hugh Holman and Sue Fields Ross (Chapel Hill, 1968), pp. 17–18.

45. Cambridge, February 10, 1921. Harvard College Library.

46. Cambridge, August 30, 1921. Harvard College Library.

47. "Written criticism of the performances, to be handed in by a date stated on each program, is a condition of membership in the regular audience of The 47 Workshop. Guests also are requested to aid in this way" (program

corded in an oft-quoted notebooks segment: "The writing of my play. Reading it to Ketchum[48]—His generous enthusiasm—alas, the *generous* enthusiasm of Baker—But how they turn on you when it fails—The coldness—the neglect."[49] In the immediate wake of this unanticipated defeat, Wolfe also drafted a letter (perhaps never sent) to George Pierce Baker, which, for the twenty-one-year-old author's flashes of developing insight, and for his moments of unregenerate humor, deserves to be cited at full length:

To fly my colors in the face of my critics may be ungracious and unbecoming. It is, assuredly, if criticism is interpretive and discerning. I cannot admit that the bulk of the last Workshop criticism was either. I must therefore write this answer, even if it is never destined to find a reader, in defense of my play.

It is not my purpose to argue my play into popularity. That, I know, is futile, and even if it were not, such shreds of pride as have been left me would prevent it. One critic asked what reason my play had for "being." If my play could not give that reason, I will not. Others found my play "painful and depressing." It grieves me to have distressed these good people. I assure them that I did not, as they seem to think, conspire to make them as uncomfortable as possible for thirty-five minutes. One person thinks the play might have been successful if the writer had had "imaginative genius"; another if he had had "something of the poet" in him. And so, if he had either, they have gone about trying to kill both.

After reading the criticisms, I feel as the tailor must have felt who was given a handful of buttons by a tramp with the instructions to please sew a suit of clothes on them. But I am at a loss just where to begin. My play has been called "depressing" so many times, and with so small an amount of illuminating evidence that it is little wonder that my wits are somewhat addled.

Some people were kind enough to give me credit for a good idea, but evidently thought I acquired it in much the fashion an ass might unearth a gold nugget with his unsuspecting hoof, and that the probability of its happening again was just as great. One auditor reminds me that William Archer no longer considers the family tie suitable material for drama,—a circumstance that should prove painful not only to me but to thousands of others who deal with triangles, divorces, domestic in-

---

note, 47 Workshop bill of October 21 and 22, 1921). Criticisms of *The Mountains* were requested "not later than October 29."

48. Arthur Ketchum, a fellow Workshop member, was the author of *The Other One*, third one-act play (Wolfe's was produced second) on the October, 1921, bill; William F. Manley, who acted the role of Richard in *The Mountains*, was the author of *The Crowsnest*, first play on this bill.

49. Harvard College Library MS *46AM-7 (25).

felicities, unhappinesses, and so on. There were others who didn't think it material for drama at all, and a great many who shuddered at what they term its "hopelessness." These are the people who would cheer Ibsen's *Ghosts!*

There were some who thought the play might have interest to a few who were familiar with the conditions it attempts to represent, but that it represents life under such peculiar circumstances that a New England audience could scarcely find an interest. This would seem to bar *The Playboy of the Western World* and the other Irish plays, the works of the Russian Theatre and the Elizabethan Drama. Yet I feel sure that our Workshop audience would not question the conditions in a Russian play, even if the characters made their entrances and exits by aeroplane.

I find solace in my defeat: a certain pleasing touch of martyrdom in my failure. There is a story of a New England minister on his way South for the first time who stood on the observation platform of his train and pitched Bibles to the heathen natives of villages of North and South Carolina, and Georgia. After a lapse of years the grateful Southland is paying its debt of gratitude. It is sending its missionaries northward. I am one of these.

The simple but distressing fact of the matter is that the average cultivated person I have met in New England can probably discourse familiarly on peasant life in Russia, Germany, or France, but lives in total darkness as to how this country lives below or beyond New York. There the world ends for them. This may be intentional: they may not care to know more about their own people—it seems they do not—but I hardly think this redounds to their credit. The most vicious menace to the literature of this country has been its tendency—particularly in New England—to "face East." During the nineteenth century we produced several men with first-class ability and third-class attainments because of this tendency. We know the result. What has been called "the Christmas card school of poetry" was the product.

Our native drama is not even yet quite beyond the imitative stage. Our dramatists—face to face with rich and inexhaustible stores of fresh characterization, pungent dialect—will fill their plays with cockney accents. We are wasting our power.[50]

Wolfe's perception here is not only incisive and sure—it is also, as Edgar Johnson once appraised Wolfe's wry portrait of the 47 Workshop crowd,[51] profound and pitiful. He had seized on this

50. Fragment, *ca.* November 1, 1921. Harvard College Library. Another letter to Baker, written at this time, is published in *Letters of Thomas Wolfe,* pp. 19–21.

51. "Thomas Wolfe and the American Dream," *A Treasury of Satire* (New York, 1945), p. 743.

instant of personal crisis and transmuted it into a cameo of satiric art.

He did not, in the bargain, dispose of the crisis. Thirteen years later, in a letter to Elizabeth Carrelle, Wolfe acknowledged: "Although the play read well in class, it was a complete and dismal failure when it was put on. No one thought it was any good, and most people took pains to tell me so. It was a very desperate occasion for me. It seemed to me that my whole life and future depended upon it. . . ."[52] In awful turmoil, lest his dramatic ambitions should be forever thwarted, he then consulted "a man on whose judgment, honesty and critical ability" he relied to the utmost, and was urged to give up playwriting, complete the Ph.D., and enter the field of teaching (much as Professor Lowes had advised him the year before).

In this mood, Wolfe doggedly set about reshaping his one-act script into full-length form: three acts and a prologue. (He had written Baker as early as August, 1921—two months prior to *The Mountains'* collision with the public—that "somehow or other my thoughts keep going back to my one-act play *The Mountains* and I feel in my heart I shall yet make a long play out of it.")[53] He toiled over this project until, by spring, he had written a prologue, two completely new acts, and an almost total revision of the original one-act script as the final act. Baker made half a dozen hurried comments on the completed manuscript—including, at one place, this prophetic query: "Aren't you anticipating your text and writing as a novelist?"[54]

In late March, Wolfe filed an application with the Harvard Appointment Office for a job teaching English and, soon after, penned a galled letter of farewell (perhaps never sent) to Baker and the 47 Workshop: "The conviction has grown on me that I shall never express myself dramatically. I am therefore ending the agony by

52. Brooklyn, N.Y., November 18, 1934. *Letters of Thomas Wolfe*, p. 427.
53. Cambridge, August 28, 1921. Harvard College Library. It is apparent from Wolfe's reference, earlier in this letter, to "my long play" that he was also at this time working on a version of the script eventually completed as *Niggertown* (*Welcome to Our City*).
54. Harvard College Library MS *46AM-7(5), Act One, p. 16, left margin alongside direction beginning "(*Mag goes out* . . .)." Cf. below p. 97.

the shortest way."[55] He did not, in the end, withdraw from Baker's course. His master of arts degree was conferred in May 1922; and he was back the next fall and completed a third year at Harvard.[56]

But he never undertook to revise or rewrite his full-length version of *The Mountains.*

THE MOUNTAINS

Wolfe's landscape in *The Mountains*, A Play in One Act, is malign, inexorable, deterministic; and Bald Pate, "*a crag . . . which . . . resembles strikingly the profile of an old, hook-nosed, sardonically grinning man,*" is the author's visible, explicit symbol for this malevolent environment. His protagonist, Richard, articulates and urgently reiterates the man-versus-nature theme, fiercely resists the mountains, then succumbs to them. There is no dualism—evidently no genuine possibility of contest. At the time of the play's conception, Wolfe was persuaded that he had written a kind of tragedy: ". . . the tragedy of this fine young man fighting against conditions that overcome him and destroy him in the end." But it was more than this. The play was meant to reflect, as well, actual conditions in the hill country of his birth: ". . . the lot of those poor oppressed mountain people, old and worn out at middle-age by their terrific hopeless battle with the mountain, . . . shutting these people eternally away from the world, hemming them in, guarding them, and finally killing them."[57] Wolfe was deeply, subjectively involved in this script, and its failure in production was a profound disappointment. He took it personally.

In transforming this nucleus into *The Mountains*, A Drama in Three Acts and a Prologue, Wolfe devised a landscape of greater dimension and complexity, and emphatically shifted the crux of causation from Bald Pate to Richard. Even in its lumpish rough state, the "full-length version" reveals unmistakably the author's capacity (under pressure) for self-discipline, his steadily improving constructive ability, and his maturing conceptual powers. The

---

55. *Letters of Thomas Wolfe*, p. 31.
56. *Welcome to Our City* was produced by the Harvard 47 Workshop on May 11, 1923. See Philip Barber, "Tom Wolfe Writes a Play," *Harper's*, CCXVI (May, 1958), 71–76.
57. See above p. 18, note 44.

synthetic determinism of the earlier version is here superseded by a dualistic dramatic universe (the hitherto static mountains symbol now balanced by the crucial, recurring train symbol); and the dramatis personae are expanded to dynastic scale (including some characters molded upon persons Wolfe had known). This unpolished work amounts to a major evolutionary step for the man who would one day write *Look Homeward, Angel*.

The germ of the one-act play is extant: a fragmentary, untitled feud script about the Travers family, evidently begun in Chapel Hill or Asheville and carried along to Harvard in the fall of 1920.[58] Richard Travers, "*a firm, slim, clean cut boy* . . . *a pure Anglo-Saxon type, blond, florid, high cheekboned*," returns home from college to his declining widower father and his nineteen-year-old sister Clara (whose name, at least, derives from Clara Paul, the twenty-one-year-old Asheville boarder with whom, in 1917, Wolfe had been briefly, deeply in love). Richard is not defined as to age or vocational bent, while Clara remains a marginal figure. Travers, essentially, is a colorless, vengeful man:

> I am an old man, my son. (*He suddenly looks old.*) I have looked forward to this meeting for weeks—and yet I've feared— I've sensed a change.
> RICHARD (*slowly*): Yes, you're right, there is a change. I see it as clearly as you.

The father, showing Richard the photograph of a younger brother, late victim of an ancient feud, cries out for retribution:

> And they must pay. By God, blood will have—
> RICHARD (*sharply*): Father! . . . Oh, the wicked stupidity of this—how useless it has been. First your older brother then your younger—then my *only* brother—and (*in a hushed voice*) and then mother. . . .

As the two now fiercely argue, we learn something of the origin of this friction between the Travers and McLurg families:

> RICHARD: . . . Forty years ago two boys were playing together—they quarreled—a little boys' quarrel I believe over a jack-knife. . . .

58. Harvard College Library MS *46AM-7(1).

Richard's efforts to reconcile his father are futile, however, and the old man sullenly inveighs against him:

> TRAVERS (*almost to himself*): And this is my reward! My son once . . . And this is what I have! (*To Richard sternly.*) Have you no sense of honor—duty? Great God, if I had known this would come about, I'd have killed you before you brought disgrace on your family name. . . .

Clara intercedes; Richard reiterates his position in lengthy, introspective speeches; and Travers orders him out of the house. A Man suddenly enters to disclose the McLurgs' murder of Jim Jackson, Richard's cousin, and to enjoin Richard and his father to get their guns and follow him:

> TRAVERS: . . . The time came quickly. (*Proudly.*) Richard, your name is Travers. (*He goes out.*) (*Clara and Richard stand as if petrified.*)
>
> CLARA (*whimpering*): Dick—Dicky—Father—alone—it is pitiful—He—

Here the script breaks off, with Richard's dilemma still unresolved.

In all respects, even allowing that it is an early sketch, this writing falls short of Wolfe's Chapel Hill folk-plays. The action is formulaic and predictable; the characters are textureless and dull; the dialogue is undifferentiated—stock speeches out of conventional stage melodrama—neither "regional" nor real; and the setting is negligible, irrelevant. Yet this was the skeleton upon which the author was to mold *The Mountains*.

In the next surviving version, to which he first assigned that title (*"The Mountains*, A Play in One Act"), Wolfe expanded his cast to six characters (Weaver—A Mountain Doctor; Richard—His Son; Laura—His Daughter; Tom Weaver—The Doctor's Brother; and Roberts and Sam—Mountaineers) and palpably conceptualized Bald Pate (". . . *a mountain peak that, at this distance, bears a striking resemblance to an old, bald-headed, sardonically grinning man*").[59]

59. Harvard College Library MS *46AM-7(3). MS *46AM-7(4) is a variant of *46AM-7(3). Dr. H. B. Weaver was a pioneer Asheville physician of Wolfe's acquaintance.

This script, performed January 25, 1921, in English 47 Workshop class, closely anticipates the version presented publicly the following fall.

Richard's attitude toward Bald Pate is here initially ambivalent, and in context momentarily disarming:

> THE YOUNG MAN (*exultantly*): The Old Man is smiling.
> THE GIRL (*startled*): The Old Man?
> THE YOUNG MAN: Bald Pate. He is glad to see me again.
> THE GIRL (*vaguely irritated*): Don't act so crazy, Dick. You
> fairly make my flesh crawl when you talk about Bald Pate smiling
> at you. It looks like eight years away from home studying to be a
> doctor would get rid of those notions. . . .

The relationship between father and son has been shaded into credibility, and the deterministic matrix strengthened, by the men's common devotion to medicine; and their ugly quarrel (of the Travers feud play) has been deleted. Tom Weaver is carefully contrasted with his brother and nephew by both dialect and demeanor (as in this passage, retained almost intact in the eventual production script):

> RICHARD: . . . And how is your—wife?
> TOM WEAVER: My wife?
> RICHARD (*confused*): Aunt Laura—I mean.
> TOM WEAVER (*spitting into the hearth*): Oh, the ole woman.
> Pshaw, Dick, thet's the sorriest crittur I ever clapped eyes on. . . .

The potential rational-versus-irrational conflict suggested by Laura's mild complaint (above) is not developed; nor does Richard, in the play's closing, obligatory scene, voice any inner struggle:

> HIS FATHER'S VOICE (*outside*): Come on, Dick, I'm waiting
> on you.
> LAURA: Go quick, they're waiting on you.
> RICHARD: That's where they get you. They can wait the
> longest. (*He goes quickly toward the door.*)
> LAURA: You are going with them?
> RICHARD: There's nothing else to do. You always go with
> them when they want you. (*He goes out.*)

LAURA (*to herself*): When they want you? (*With sudden understanding.*) The Mountains.

Laura, in crisis, remains complacent and uncomprehending, and Richard, for all his earlier earnest idealism, ends up a passive victim. As the vague "they" and "them" of the hero's concluding speeches are ultimately ambiguous, Laura's curtain-line enunciation of "The Mountains" is supererogatory, not emphatic.

Wolfe envisioned at this stage "an honest, true, and in places, powerful piece of work," but he had not achieved it. His Richard is languid, undefined, and unappealing (we are not likely to care whether he lives or dies); while Bald Pate, as deterministic force, seems so only narrowly and intermittently, within the protagonist's romantic imagination. The author's identification and involvement with the protagonist are part of his writing problem—for Richard is clearly a tentative projection of Thomas Wolfe (as is Tom Weaver). In extenuation, one may plead that Richard is a primitive paradigm of the similarly hillbound and provincial hero of later Wolfe fiction; but the anticipation of Eugene-George is indeed faint.

The lengthy stage direction (over three pages, single-spaced) prefacing Wolfe's revised one-act script of *The Mountains* is detailed, compact, and illuminating. The scene, generalized as "*a Mountain District in the Western Part of North Carolina,*" obliquely implies mountain-ringed Asheville and its environs; and the living-room setting, evocative *of "some subtle reflection of the personalities of fine but opposite people who have lived here,"* embodies a transmuted recollection of the author's boyhood Asheville residence.[60] Wolfe subjectively posits a room "*rich in its mixture of strength and sweetness . . . a sober pensive tone almost of melancholy, but not of gloom*" and, in the distance, "*a mountain land-*

---

60. Cf. *Look Homeward, Angel*, p. 192: "The fusion of two strong egotisms, Eliza's inbrooding and Gant's expanding outward, made of him a fanatical zealot in the religion of chance." The vividly described (but extraneous, and later deleted) iron match-safe, "*a very knowing looking iron sparrow, inviting the touch on his back that will make him dive like a shot into the box and bring up a match impaled on his long beak,*" is probably a stubborn relic of Wolfe's childhood. The "*large wooden clock,*" likewise superfluous to this play's action, is recurrent in Wolfe's late, posthumously published story "The Return of the Prodigal."

scape: The view could not be called 'peaceful.' It is mighty in its great repose and full of power and quiet depth." He has here deliberately transcended the technical restrictions of dramatic form and (as Professor Baker was to remonstrate) is "anticipating your text and writing as a novelist."[61]

Wolfe's Richard of this version is ". . . *of medium height and slight figure. He moves with a swift, erect sureness that gives authority and dignity to his bearing. His face is thin, but its features are strong and finely drawn, his eyes are dark and brooding and set far back in his head, his movements are quick and nervous, and when he talks he uses his whole body."* But these externals—a derivative, vaguely Byronic stereotype—are irrelevant to the inward self-portrait of the author. When he writes that Richard *"is a talkative, imaginative young man, given to boomerang speculations which end where they start too often, and return to plague their author,"* we notice the involuntary Shakespearean paraphrase (anticipating a recurrent tendency in Wolfe's fiction); and in the ensuing comment that *"Restraint, compromise, or the path generally called 'the middle way' are held in contempt by Richard"* we perceive a tentative formulation of Wolfe's own evolving ethos. In his explication of that ethos, we discern the Hegelian philosophy (and distinctive nomenclature) of Horace Williams: *"He* [Richard] *can visualize only two forces in life: a spirit that seeks truth and one that denies it. Life to him means a conflict between these two. This is dualism, if you like. Richard knows of only one way to absorb his negations: that is to forget them and conquer them— or be conquered."*[62]

In Wolfe's further assertion that Richard *". . . can visualize evil or good as forces as intense and tangible as a mystic of the Middle Ages; this requires imagination, and its fusing spirit runs like a flame through all the processes of his inner life,"* we read not only

---

61. Cf. above p. 21, note 54.
62. Cf. A. L. S., Wolfe to Edwin Greenlaw, Cambridge, Mass., March, 1922, Harvard College Library: "I have the utmost difficulty in bringing into my mind the picture of Professor Williams absorbing a negation (Confidential)"; "O Lost," Harvard College Library MS *46AM-7(25), III, 973: "How do we come to Truth? By making our lives prevail. How do we make our lives prevail? By absorbing the moment of Negation."

an objectification of his hero's capacity to conceptualize Bald Pate, but a hopeful affirmation as well of the young author's own artistic aspirations. The focus is upon poetry, not science. Thus, Wolfe's succeeding elaboration of Richard-as-doctor is extraneous, novelesque, unrealized dramatically:

As a man of medicine, and a scientist, his possibilities are incalculable. Most of the classmates who have recently graduated from medical college with him will go out and be fine, honest gentlemen, and a credit to their profession,—steady, earnest, and useful men. But from Richard you can expect more than this. He will tell you that he can see God through a microscope; and, without his telling you, you would know he can see beauty and unity in the vast things of Nature,—or, perhaps, something malignant and evil there. He has the capacity for work, and yet, time and again, the things his classmates sweated to know came to him in one blinding flash of light. As he grows older and wiser he will use this same quality on men, and much of the beauty and the tragedy and the mystery in the hearts of men will be revealed to his deeper insight, to thrill and exalt him. It has been his fate, and it will continue to be his lot, to struggle with the Angel of Vision; but from that uneven contest may emerge, if nothing destructive happens, a spirit that can look serenely through the rags of the world about him and still see that which is real and eternal. If this seems too eulogistic, we can reply that it fails in adequately conveying the fineness of Richard.

It is difficult not to read autobiography into this extended narrative. Depending on one's respective disposition toward the author's mature writing, the foregoing passage will appear either prolix and nakedly presumptuous, or else lyrical and darkly prophetic. Richard's age is nowhere explicitly stated (though we may confidently compute it to be twenty-five): Thomas Wolfe, at the time of this play's writing, was twenty-one.

Neither Laura nor Dr. Weaver is so minutely characterized as the protagonist. Neither figure is ever quite drawn into ethical focus; and neither, therefore, is likely to elicit our interest or sympathy. We are far more likely to remember and respond to Tom Weaver and Aunt Mag, both of whose roles are more sharply defined. Roberts (who recurs briefly in chapter three of *The Web and the Rock*) here affords a theatrically arresting alternation of pathos and menace; while Sam, the four-speech mountaineer *nuntius*, is a strictly peripheral part.

The author may have intended in Laura an idealized Clara Paul, or he may have abandoned this possibility with his uncompleted, untitled Travers family feud script. Whatever Wolfe's intentions, they did not produce a palpable sister for Richard; and this deficiency is manifest in the opening stage direction:

Laura comes up through the hall and enters the room. She is a small, beautifully moulded girl of twenty-two with dark, mobile features and a flashing crown of brown hair. She goes over to the table and absently rearranges the books, moves restlessly to the window and looks out for a moment, then returns to the hearth, where she stands for a moment gazing at the portrait. She drums nervously on the mantel with her fingers and returns to the table and seats herself there. She selects a book at random and thumbs the pages indifferently.

Laura's mute indecisiveness here (though it prefigures her conduct later in the play) is not yet dramatic action: her aimless business of books, window, portrait, and mantel merely betray the apprentice author's technical incapacity. Wolfe haltingly defers the start of his play until Richard's entrance; and Laura, fumbled at the outset, rapidly dwindles into the hero's neutral *raisonneur.*

Dr. Weaver, whom we might expect to figure as Richard's spiritual antagonist, fares little better. Wolfe's initial description of him is disarming: "*Dr. Weaver is a heavy, florid-faced man of medium height and slightly over fifty years old. He is smooth-shaven and his hair is short and grizzly gray. His face is seamed with heavy decisive lines which do not detract, however, from his genial, good-humored features. The total impression from the man is one of kindness linked to strength and character.*" But Dr. Weaver's early assertion that " . . . all the education in the world can't change the fact of kith and kin" signals his prior capitulation to clan—it quite belies the author's claims for his "*kindness linked to strength and character.*" Notwithstanding his miscellaneous reported past philanthropies, Dr. Weaver ultimately proves to be tribesman first and humanitarian perhaps. Richard's debate, when it comes, is not with his father at all—it is with his Uncle Tom.

"Pa's a good man, Dick. We'll never know a better," Laura pleads, early in the play. "But he couldn't go against his family. Don't you see it's hopeless?" Her next lines emphasize Tom Weaver's dominating role in this play and foreshadow Richard's impending submission to clan and to the mountains: "Why, Uncle Tom has looked forward to your coming back all this time. It has never occurred to him that you might be changed. He can't see anything else in life but a fight with the Gudgers. Every week he comes in and oils your rifle till it fairly shines. And when he puts it back in the closet he always says: 'Just wait till Dick gets home, we'll show them a thing or two.' That's what you've got to face, Dick."

Wolfe introduces Richard's uncle in general terms, as ". . . *a typical mountaineer,—a man of forty-five, but apparently older. He is lean to gauntness, his tall bony frame is stooped, his long arms dangling to his knees.*" Tom Weaver, importantly, bears the author's first name and shares his outward physical features. He needs none of the rationalized narrative detail here lavished upon Richard (as, to a lesser extent, upon Dr. Weaver), for he emerges through dialogue and action as the script's most compelling dramatic creation. Uncle Tom, unregenerate Carolina provincial, is idealist Richard's irrepressible alter-ego and the focal character through whom, as boy and man, the author was to link the disparate units of his succeeding full-length script. He is the "dark side" of Thomas Wolfe.

Despite "*the unmeasured chasm in education and training*" that distinguishes Tom Weaver from his doctor brother, Wolfe pointedly comments that "*they seem to recognize no difference here, they are natural, unaffected and entirely at their ease with each other.*" Mag Weaver, by contrast, is keenly self-conscious of that chasm; and when Tom calls to tell her that they are staying for supper, she is embarrassed: "(*outside,—shrill, cracked and strident* [*voice*]) Law me! I hain't fit to be seen in company." The author's description of her is poignant: "*She is a hard unlovely looking creature, her sallow skin is stretched tightly over her sharp, bony face, her wispy hair has been pulled back painfully and fastened in a knot behind; from the corner of her mouth protrudes a small stick; her mouth is discolored with snuff at the edges. She is dressed in gingham which fits her shapeless body tightly; she moves awkwardly and is deeply embarrassed by the presence of so much unaccustomed luxury in her surroundings.*"

In the earlier version of this play, produced in 47 Workshop class, Tom Weaver's wife is Aunt Laura (mentioned only once[63] and not presented as a character), a name affectionately borrowed from Wolfe's Aunt Laura Westall (Mrs. Henry A. Westall), in whose nearby Medford, Massachusetts, home he was then a frequent visitor.[64] It is problematical whether he may also have borrowed some antecedents of character from Mrs. Westall, in devising Mag Weaver; but Wolfe's impulse for drawing upon immediate, personal experience for literary materials is already manifest.[65] His sympathy for Aunt Mag is unmistakable. Though deprived of formal schooling, she demonstrates shrewd native intelligence and, ironically, seems to possess the highest level of metaphysical awareness in the play. With admirable dramatic instinct, the apprentice author assigned to Aunt Mag the function of Chorus.

In later life, Wolfe professed to have "a mountaineer's suspicion of people from outside;"[66] and the portrait of Richard's mother, "*a woman, frail and extraordinarily beautiful, dressed in the manner of thirty years ago*," was meant to stand in this play for "people from outside." It is apparent that the author intended this portrait to be both emphatic and symbolic. The mother's fate was supposed to foreshadow her son's; and Wolfe's hero early implants the note of foreboding in our consciousness: "When I was four or five years old I can remember—mother . . . sitting here by the hearth night after night rocking away with me in her arms. . . . Laura, I know it was the eternal fear of that waiting that killed her."

63. See above p. 25.
64. Cf. fragment of a letter, Wolfe to Frank C. Wolfe (his eldest brother), Cambridge, Mass., early summer, 1921 (*Letters of Thomas Wolfe*, p. 15): "He [our Uncle Henry] and Aunt Laura are a great pair; they are giving me materials for a great play which I shall write some day. . . . Aunt Laura spends a great part of the time in telling me what a fearful handicap it is to be born a Westall, how I must watch myself at every point to keep the family traits from cropping out, and what an unbalanced, lopsided clan we are in general."
65. Cf. *You Can't Go Home Again*, pp. 96–97: "Mark Joyner [and] Mag, his wife. . . ."
66. Nowell, *Thomas Wolfe: A Biography*, p. 12. Cf. Paul L. Benjamin, "The Carolina Playmakers," *The Survey*, XLVIII (1922), 436: "[North Carolina] is a state of native birth with an infusion of less than 2 per cent of those of foreign birth or parentage."

If we demur at the implausibility of Richard's outburst, we may also incline to overlook Tom Weaver's helpful, objective statement, further on, that " . . . one day he [Richard's father] turned up bringin' the purtiest gal back from the city I ever clapped eye on." The crucial element is "city"—unspecified as to northern or southern (for the conflict is not sectional), yet suggestive of the play's underlying economic dynamics. William F. Kennedy has emphasized that the mature Wolfe, in his novels, achieved "a high degree of freedom from the bias of his social class and economic interests;"[67] and we notice that the apprentice Wolfe, in *The Mountains*, imaginatively anticipated historian C. Vann Woodward's assertion that: "In spite of the spectacular rise of completely new cities in an old section of the country and the growth of many old ones in the last two decades of the century, the sum total of urbanization in the South was relatively unimportant. . . . The Southern people remained, throughout the rise of the 'New South,' overwhelmingly a country people, by far the most rural section of the Union."[68]

It is not Tom Weaver and the unseen Gudgers and Fitzpatricks who here embody this rural-country principle, but city-civilized Dr. Weaver, Richard, and Laura. When Richard expresses pity for mountaineers like the man who broke his leg trying to fly like a bird, therefore, his father soberly reminds him: "They're your own people, son. You came from that stock." Richard's superstitious awe of the mountains is shared by his otherwise matter-of-fact Uncle Tom: "Hit'll git me some day, creepin' down on me a few feet a year. Son, I've gone out into my back yard o'nights when no one was lookin' an' cussed that damn mountain with every dirty name I could think of." The uncle and nephew's mutually

67. "Economic Ideas in Contemporary Literature—The Novels of Thomas Wolfe," *Southern Economic Journal*, XX (July, 1953), 50.
68. *Origins of the New South* (Baton Rouge, 1951), p. 139. Cf. Ralph McGill, "The South's Glowing Horizon—If. . . ," *Saturday Review*, LI, x (March 9, 1968), 22: "The change from rural-agrarian to urban-industrial has been rapid but spotty. It is not yet complete." Of the mature novelist, however, Paschal Reeves has emphasized: "Wolfe was an urban writer despite his dream to portray 'the whole web of life and of America.' The rural areas are seen only in fleeting glimpses from the windows of a train while he was in transit from one urban oasis to another," *Thomas Wolfe's Albatross: Race and Nationality in America* (Athens, 1968), p. 14.

irrational response to the mountains is significant: it confirms Dr. Weaver's remonstrance. The play's cultural-ethical polarity, in conception, is urban-education-rational (the mother's portrait) versus rural-ignorance-irrational (the mountains); but the portrait, if Wolfe had meant it to serve as symbol for the former, remained a static symbol, one which failed to materialize dramatically. In expanding *The Mountains* to full-length form, the author was to present Richard's mother—named Laura—palpably as character and to enrich and strengthen the symbolic structure with a new, dynamic element: the train.

"It is not the tragedy of Richard, which seems so big to many people, but the effect of natural forces on the human soul, as you say, that I want to emphasize," Wolfe wrote to Baker late in the revision process. "Individual tragedy seems small to me by comparison."[69] He also told his mentor:

When one writes a play one feels there are a thousand ways of saying a thing and that one usually selects the worst. But when one rewrites the play it is found that a very definite mould has been formed which it is difficult to break. I believe I have broken the mould in the last act— whether for good or ill I dare not say. Not once in the writing have I referred to the original one act. The introduction of the romance element will not cheapen the thing, I hope. I did it not to popularize the piece but to make a more living figure of the girl, Laura, who was somewhat wooden before. It will be said, I know, that a love affair with a member of the opposing clan is a somewhat conventional device but all plotting is somewhat conventional and I can not see why the device is not a good one if I have made a true and honest lover of Will Gudger and a more human figure of the girl Laura "torn between" (as the saying goes) love for her beaten father and the blunt young apple grower. . . .

If nothing else, the chastened tyro had learned humility and restraint; for this letter (whether or not ever dispatched) signals his now disciplined sensitivity to audience reaction. But the full-length version, for all Wolfe's brooding reservations, compellingly channels and focuses "the effect of natural forces." We also discover

69. Undated fragment (rough draft), in folder with scenario and partial drafts of full-length *The Mountains*. Harvard College Library MS *46AM-7(2).

that he has indeed "broken the mould" of the one-act script with the new play's opening scene.

In his earlier script, the basis of the longstanding quarrel is land —"a dispute over a boundary line" (compactly disclosed late in the action):

> TOM WEAVER: One day ole man Fitzpatrick come on yore Grandaddy fencin' his land an' he said: "Who gave ye leave to fence my land?" Yore Grandaddy said: "Who said hit was yore land?" Ole man Fitzpatrick yells: "I say so, by God!" "You don't need to git so hot about hit," yore Grandaddy says. "Thar ain't no call to go gittin' on yore head 'bout hit." Ole man Fitzpatrick goes off but he comes back in 'bout an hour with a gun. He don't come close but he yells, "We'll see now if ye don't git off, damn ye!" an' he shoots at yore Grandaddy.
>
> RICHARD: And he killed him?
>
> TOM WEAVER (*with satisfaction*): No, damn him, he didn't. Yore Grandaddy laid fer him an' shot him two weeks atter he was comin' from meetin'. . . . Kill him deader'n a nail.

Three features especially warrant notice here: first, the sharply differentiated regional speech (more pronounced here, as "reported," than elsewhere in the dialogue); second, the effective exposition through dramatic narration (Tom Weaver's vivid re-enactment); and third, the author's subtle balancing of ethical ambiguity (Fitzpatrick had shot first, but Richard's grandfather had killed him in cold blood).

In the revised, expanded treatment, Tom Weaver is advanced from incidental reporter of these events to peripheral participant in them; since, in the Prologue, he is first presented to us as an impressionable boy of fourteen. The Prologue's opening stage directions and pantomime are intentionally elaborate, beyond practicably realizable scale; yet their every element is purposefully dramatic, evoking an atmosphere of isolation and futility. The poor and stony soil, "*of a clayey color like the weather-baked skins of the fence builders*," is emblematic of the two mute workers' enslavement to this land; while the boy's restless activity ("*a lively fellow . . . looks up at the crows with interest, listening attentively when he hears the cowbells, . . . picks up a stone and hurls it down the hill* . . . ") correspondingly suggests the inherent possibility of choice. Talk of jugs and Jugtown and the distant train whistle both imply the different, yet more complex world beyond this hillside—and we are led to sense the boy's vague yearning toward that other world:

> TOMMY: Whar do the cyars go, Gran'paw?
>
> GRAN'PAW (*with the same indefinite gesture*): Out thar. . . .
>
> TOMMY: I'd like to ride on the cyars.

The boy's mild father is named Ben (for Wolfe's beloved brother, who had died late in 1918); and the elder Gudger seems also to have had an Asheville prototype (Gudgers abound in *Look Homeward, Angel*[70]). The former, a rational but ineffectual ameliorist, pleads the worthlessness of the disputed ground: "Hit's mighty pore land anyway. Hit won't raise beans. Mountain land!" And Gudger's temperate complaint is, likewise, eminently just: "I don't grudge yore usin' the spring. Use hit an' welcome, same's you allus done. But ye're fencin' in my land now an' that ain't right."

But Old Weaver, rejecting all entreaties, provokes Gudger to discharge the fatal shot. As the old man falls, "*the jug is overturned and broken;*" and at final curtain, while Tommy looks on in horror, "*the train whistle blows far off.*" Both the broken jug and distant train are meant to symbolize the boy's missed opportunity for escape; and if the apprentice dramatist's figural method seems too subtle to carry in performance (as is probably the case), one may at least credit the attempt.

Wolfe's vaunted Prologue is certainly several cuts above mere melodrama—for the play's deterministic mechanism is here set in motion as motivated retribution, rather than (as hitherto) instinctive or mindless violence. Tom Weaver the man is movingly, pitifully, ironically forecast in Tom Weaver the boy. So, too, are the divergent destinies of his son Sam and his nephew Richard. (Wolfe

70. Cf. "Brock or Saul Gudger," p. 72; "Saul Gudger," p. 179; "Dick Gudger, the agent" (who sells Dixieland to W. O. Gant), p. 128; "Randolph Gudger, the bank president," p. 472; "Nan [and Mary] Gudger . . . and two brothers, hulking young thugs of twenty and eighteen years, who always bore upon their charmed bodies fresh knifewounds, blue lumps and swellings, and other marks of their fights in poolroom and brothel. They lived in a two-story shack of rickety lumber on Clingman Street," pp. 146–47.

afterwards translated his vivid scene of Old Weaver, Tommy, and the passing train into the vignette of a Jersey fisherman and his son which opens Chapter Thirteen of *The Web and the Rock*.)

Despite its workmanlike design, Act One is theatrically the least effective section of this play: it is overlong, patently schematic, and dull. Wolfe has largely rationalized, rather than dramatized, factors motivating Dr. Weaver's choice of clan over his wife and children; and what he must have planned as exposition and fore-shadowing of Richard's final-act dilemma dissipates, rather than enhances, our interest in the yet unseen protagonist.

Idealist-positivist Weaver, though ethically bested by his skeptic-pessimist father-in-law in their rambling epistemological debate (21 typescript pages), persists in his stubborn resolve to remain among "my people." Through the agency of coarse, backward Bessie Smathers, whose mountaineer's pride causes her baby's death, and whose senseless loyalty to a philandering moonshiner husband precisely parallels Weaver's own dubious dedication, we realize that the young doctor's "imperative" is at base irrational. Yet Weaver imposes this precipitant decision upon his compliant out-lander wife. Mrs. Weaver, like Dickens' pathetic Paul Dombey, was formulaically created in order to die; though Wolfe's fore-doomed doctor's wife is never brought to life—she is neither affecting in this act nor subsequently lamented (if even missed).

The social and economic realities underlying Bessie's fierce, fatal pride and Mag's tense relations with her employer (both implying a distinct rural caste structure) interest us more; so does the serio-comic innovation of Tom Weaver's grotesque courtship doggerel (prefiguring the admired gravestone doggerel of *Look Homeward, Angel*). And Wolfe's subtle handling of his central, opposing mountain and train symbols is admirable. This time his stage directions closely juxtapose " . . . *the occasional sound of cowbells . . . the sound of a springless wagon jolting slowly over a rough road* [and] *a glimpse of polished steel rails running along the flank of the hill*"—imaginatively suggesting a flux of pastoral, rural, and industrial elements that lends both background and animating force to his dramatic action.

The train is now actual and immediate: its laborious, twenty-minute mountainside climb to the station is emphasized, and we hear its roar and watch its lights flash by as it bears Dr. Davis past Weaver's house, northward and away. But this resourceful stage-craft only undergirds the train's metaphysical implication: dynamic emblem of pragmatic man against nature, or (more narrowly, here) escape. Dr. Davis urges this point forcefully to Weaver toward the close of their debate: "The world is going by you outside these hills; it goes by you twice a day when the trains come in. If you stay you are lost, lost!" Weaver, however, subjectively relates to the mountains in dual terms of permanence and transcience (some-what as Wolfe would later present the river symbol in his George Webber novels):

Man is a proud, swift being capable of moving mountains. Then he decays and is senile and weak and old. We grow strong to sicken and die. When we think we're learning to live, we're learning to die. That is the process of growth. And the mountains remain. They can't grow at all; they can't add even an inch to their stature. There's something splendid about that. Eternal, changeless mountains. The victory is ul-timately yours. If winter comes, the spring will bring you youth again. So, like the gods, they grow old only to be young again.

Yet Weaver's deterministic dualism is not Wolfe's, for the author had implanted the germ of The Mountains' ethical resolution—fog —early in this act: " . . . ghostly mists through which the eye can-not pierce." (In the play's final scene, as the train pushes at last past the rockslide, this shroud of mountain fog will lift.)

Wolfe's selective use of Platonic natural analogy in Act One is eloquent and impressive. The act begins "toward sundown of a day late in September" and ends with the sun's red glow gradually de-clining into darkness: "Bessie goes out. It seems much darker within the room. The lamp on the table is wholly insufficient to combat the darkness. The Night that surrounds the house is impenetrable and black. Weaver stands shaded in semi-darkness looking out of the window." Weaver, who had brought his bride here in spring, has promised to leave with her at the next coming of spring; but at Bessie's departure he exclaims: "Did you ever see a darker night? You should have seen his face! His mouth was closed tighter than ever. He made no noise, she said. He was a good soldier. He had— courage. That's a big thing." In a now figurative context, Night not only embodies death, but—with Weaver's perverse transferral of his own rationalized values to Bessie's dead child—connotes resignation and defeat.

Catastrophe is imminent in his ensuing impulsive and coercive injunction: "You wouldn't leave me now! You wouldn't leave me now!" Mrs. Weaver instantly intuits all; and her reassurance is vitiated by a wounded outcry: "Oh, why did you say that?" The sound of her father's train, then faintly heard, signals an ethical alternative that Weaver has forfeited.

Act Two, roughly one-third the length of Act One, shifts the focus to Tom Weaver's rural foothills cabin, "*a large untidy room . . . used . . . for eating, sleeping and the preparation of food.*" The author alludes sympathetically to Tom's "*painful advance in the world*" and his "*increased dignity of position*"; and notice is taken of "*various lithographs of religious nature on the walls.*"[71] The setting—"*walls . . . blackened by years of smoke . . . draughty chimney . . . small window . . . rude table . . . delapidated cupboard*"— bears mute witness to Tom's unequal struggle with the mountains, at whose base his makeshift house perilously stands. And Tom's imprint is upon his family: their harsh regional dialect sets them starkly apart from the cultivated town Weavers.

Sam's "*keen, intelligent face and sombre, smouldering eyes*" and his fervid yearning toward town, as they remind us of his father in earlier years (the Prologue), hint at the operation of some recurring cycle of futility:

> TOM WEAVER: He's got some such notion, I reckon. All boys his age git hit. I had hit myself when I was young.

A hopeful prospect is briefly entertained of Sam's accompanying young Richard northward for an education. Mag doggedly affirms her son's aspiration against Tom's stormy objections, and Dr. Weaver agrees to finance the venture. But the boy's escape is precipitantly thwarted by natural forces: " *. . . the sliding of sand and*

---

71. They include ". . . *a representation of Our Lord seated on a cloud, surrounded by a legion of white and black angels and black and white cherubs. The inscription reads: 'God loves them both.'*" Cf. *Look Homeward, Angel*, p. 305: ". . . a religious motto in flowered scrollwork, framed in walnut: *God Loves Them Both.*"

gravel down the slope . . . quickly increases in amount and fury until it rises above the sound of the rain."

The mountains, bearing down upon Tom Weaver's house and crops, now assume the aspect of a relentless devouring force; for Wolfe has here expanded imaginative symbol into awesome actuality. Sam's selfless decision at this point to remain at home—"He's right. I can't go."—both parallels Dr. Weaver's prior choice at the end of Act One and anticipates young Richard's dilemma of the final act.

Wolfe's feud motif, ominous but unobtrusive in Act One, is skillfully integrated and developed in Act Two—as not only the two elder Weaver brothers clash, but also their respective sons. Both Sam and young Richard have sought to conciliate younger members of the Gudger clan and, for their pains, are rebuked by Sam's sullen, uncomprehending brother Reese. Dr. Weaver attempts to ameliorate the conflict; but Richard first challenges his uncle, then, *"with unthinking boylike brutality,"* turns on his father: "If I go off and come back here when I'm a doctor I don't have to do like you've done, pa." Richard, here poised between just indignation and rash over-confidence, emerges unmistakably as focal character for the action to come; and such is now the momentum of this play that we are not likely to cavil at his irrational inveighing against mountains as though against some cosmic evil force.

"Sundown of a day in early summer . . . misty redness through smoky storm clouds at the horizon's edge" (initial stage directions of Act Three) ironically forecasts the outcome of Richard's impending crisis. As his father's earlier capitulation was implicit in *"toward sundown . . . autumn"* (opening stage directions of Act One), so Richard's is prefigured here. Wolfe has employed iterative natural analogy (and selective pathetic fallacy) in Acts One and Three both as narrative device and as vehicle for his play's thematic and structural principle of recurring cycle.

But while Richard of the one-act script had been a pathetic victim, a conventional romantic hero, Richard of the revised play is such only in his own fatalistic self-image. Wolfe's more mature, more complex scheme is figuratively advanced in three further elements—his paired symbols of mountain and train, and the fog: " . . . *the upper parts of the mountains are cloaked in thick, grey mists. At intervals there comes from the distance the hoarse blasts of a train whistle, which appears neither to advance nor to recede.*" The nearer sounds of "*a banjo being picked, accompanied by the heavy thump of boots and uneven drunken voices,*" moreover, signify Wolfe's extension of the play's conflict onto a societal plane. His concern is now with community, not alone with Weavers, Gudgers, and Fitzpatricks.

After an interval of several years, Sam—"*a lean, browned, not unattractive appearing young mountaineer of four and twenty*"— is weary of his family's still losing battle with mud and rain, bitter at his missed chance of schooling, and (with a fresh outbreak of feuding) anxious for Richard's safety. Sam's tense conversation with Laura (a new character) and her brother, just returned from college, is counterpointed by shouts and cries of the drunken men and whistle blasts from the slide-blocked train. In marked contrast to his one-act script's sluggish early exposition, Wolfe has here skillfully compounded a variety of dramatic means to build suspense and thrust his action forward.

The pace slackens momentarily into "too much mere talk" (Baker's marginal note[72]) following Sam's departure, with first Richard and Laura's poignant but static exchange about mountaineers (". . . shut in and crushed down from the cradle to the grave") and then Richard and Dr. Weaver's nostalgic, déjà vu dialogue about frustrated idealism ("Today I'm an old man . . . and most of [my] fine schemes were wrecked years ago"). Interest quickens with the advent of Will Gudger, member of the rival clan and Laura's gentle orchardist suitor.

Will bears news of the mob gathering at the store, Tom Weaver's feverish recruitment of armed men, and the clearing of the rail lines; and he urgently implores Laura to take the train with him to Stanton and marry him: "Then we'll take a trip North. If there's trouble here they can howl and rave all they want to, but I shan't bring you back to it." (The formality, indeed stiffness, of Will's

72. Typescript, p. 14, opposite Richard's speech beginning "Poor woman!" Cf. below p. 152.

speech—we notice "shan't"—is a mark of his breeding; both his refined language and attachment to his apple trees are meant to set
his character and to elicit our esteem.) Confronted with Laura's
vague objections ("Oh, Will, I've been so close to pa") and Richard's plea for moderation ("I think tomorrow would be better"),
however, Will reluctantly departs; and the way is clear for Richard's showdown with Tom Weaver.

But this obligatory scene, when it comes, is relatively subdued.
Tom's entreaties alone have little effect upon either Richard or his
father; for Wolfe has saved back Sam's murder as precipitating,
impelling factor. Richard, incredulous that his doctor father should
neglect Roberts' ailing daughter, at first tries to dissuade him from
joining the avengers; but, failing this, he presently turns Roberts
away and joins them himself:

> It's those accursed mountains. They never let go.
> (*A train whistle blows nearby.*)
> ... I was a prophet in the wilderness too soon. The moun-
> tains aren't ready to receive prophets.

As Laura and Mag stand by, choric and passive, Richard then hurries after his uncle and father; and the play ends with sounds of the
train sweeping past, Laura's plaintive lament, and nearby rifle shots.

From Wolfe's emphatic closing juxtaposition of Mag's "The
train got through" and Laura's "The world went by" we are to
understand that Richard's conduct in crisis is deliberate and wrong
—conscious moral choice, not implacable mechanistic design. Dr.
Weaver offers an explicit analogy, early in Act Three, between
Richard and the train: "You belong to the new order. And the
track is clear for you." And Laura, against Richard's resigned,
brooding reflections on fog-shrouded Bald Pate, pointedly ob-
serves: "The fog is lifting, Dick." But immediately afterward,
Richard joins the very mob he so vehemently deplores. By means
of the dissipated fog and the unblocked train, the author symboli-
cally counterpoints Richard's ethical blindness and willful inertia.[73]

73. Cf. *Welcome to Our City*, in *Esquire*, XLVIII (October, 1957), 83:
"*It grows darker. The lamps in the street go on. There is a fog in Altamont,
and it drifts across the street, before the windows, like crimson smoke.*"
There is little chance that (thus buried in the final stage directions) Wolfe's

Wolfe had settled for determinism in his one-act version of *The Mountains;* here, he has attempted tragedy.

This is not to say Wolfe achieved his lofty aspiration—either formally or metaphysically. Both scripts are exercises—apprentice-work toward his eventual ripening as a writer of fiction. Their mutually circular pattern and pervasive symbolism are marks of developing talent and conscious craftsmanship, but not of genius. Viewed in strict terms of theatrical effectiveness, neither play really succeeds, since each was too abstractly conceived. This is a curious shortcoming, in a writer whose great agony in mature years would arise from impugned formlessness.

In neither script is Richard clearly differentiated from his father, nor is either character convincingly motivated in his choice of community over conscience. Wolfe has adequately objectified his theme of regional provincialism, but he has not compellingly dramatized it. (This task he was to accomplish as novelist, notably in *Look Homeward, Angel,* and *You Can't Go Home Again,* where narrative focus is sustained upon his respective protagonists.)

The maudlin allusions to Richard's dead mother and Dr. Weaver's graphic details of mountaineer Tom Bryce's family are peripheral to the main action of his one-act script; and, as the play's most affecting characterization is lavished upon Tom Weaver and Mag, the more central figures of Richard, Laura, and Dr. Weaver are stinted. At final curtain, Mag's plaintive, elegiac "I reckon thar ain't no way o' findin' out" (reminiscent of Synge's and O'Casey's bereft rural/urban women) briefly moves us, as the ostensible young hero probably does not. Wolfe's deterministic mountains symbol is ingenious, but in the last analysis superficial: if Richard is convinced of it, we are not.

The author went on to establish in the Prologue of his expanded

---

symbolic implication would carry in performance. Less practicable still (in theatrical terms) is his concatenation of metaphor in *Mannerhouse*'s elaborate final *post-curtain* stage directions (New York, 1948), p. 183: "*There is heard immediately a terrific crash and the sounds of heavy timbers, which buckle and settle. There is a lesser reverberation, followed by silence, save for the faint far ending of a waltz which dies upon the wind; save for a merciless little drop of water which somewhere swells, develops, and falls at length with punctual, unvarying monotony.* A THIN VOICE *faint and far* Snap your fingers, gentlemen."

version that these mountains (*i.e.*, the land) were neutral, not evil, and that the fatal quarrel had originated in human materialism. Ben serves here as ethical norm; and the train whistle and Tommy's susceptibility imply the efficacy of individual choice. Wolfe's Hegelian mentor Horace Williams had put it similarly: "If the individual has the quality of 'faith' he can then 'remove mountains.' No quantity is beyond the quality when the identity of the two is seen. . . . The content of life is changed. The reality is no more a Beyond to be longed for in the imagination through the emotions, but a Truth to be grasped in the intelligence, a law to be illustrated in action, a beauty in perfection to be present in the life."[74] If we recognize the Prologue's paired mountains and train symbols (plus the broken jug), we may view the play's recurring frustrated escape motif objectively, thus ironically. We are to notice that Dr. Weaver (and his wife), in Act One; Sam Weaver, in Act Two; then Will Gudger (also Laura), and finally Richard, in Act Three, each contemplates "escape" by train but does not leave. Wolfe's dominant symbols are now integral, and his structure is distinct.

But will the playgoer likely discern the Prologue's subtly submerged metaphor? Crucial as such poetic details are (and the careful reader will find them), Wolfe has not raised these aspects to palpable theatricality. They do not work. Nor, in terms of continuity, do the ensuing three acts. Even if one successfully bridges the decade between Prologue and Act One, he will sense Wolfe's failure to connect the disparate elements of *The Mountains'* major units. In Tom Weaver, his richest and roundest character of both scripts, he almost succeeded. Richard's Uncle Tom dramatically foreshadows blind, usurious Rumford Bland, whose ominous query

74. *The Evolution of Logic*, pp. 62–63. Cf. Williams, *Logic for Living*, pp. 48, 53–54: "I want it understood that I stand for the integrity of the individual. But what happens when you analyze the individual? You will be astonished to see how you dissolve into the traits of your mother, father, and grandfather. [The individual] gradually becomes independent of his environment and becomes self-sufficient. The life that is not dependent is the spiritual life. When the object, the individual, becomes spiritual it becomes independent. . . . Reality is spiritual. That is, it is not dependent on the environment." Predictably, Williams stressed (p. 228): "The greatest thing about Hegel is the dialectic process. The antagonism between form and action gives way to a unity where form and action meet on a higher level. . . ."

to George Webber, "Do you think you can go home again?" affords the title to Wolfe's last novel.[75]

Act One contains two important characters, Dr. Davis and Mrs. Weaver, not seen in the succeeding acts; while young Richard, projected as the author's focal character, is yet a child—mentioned but unseen. Act Two, fully a generation later, proffers a new locale, new characters, and new events; and though we at last meet Richard, the center of interest here is Sam (a nonentity in the one-act script, but now Tom Weaver's teen-age son). Act Three compounds these deficiencies: it requires another several years' hiatus, again shifts the setting, introduces new characters, and divides its dramatic focus three ways (Will Gudger's courtship, Sam Weaver's death, Richard's dilemma). Instead of selecting and developing a single figure (Tom Weaver, Sam Weaver, or Richard might have served) through one sustained action, Wolfe has simply repeated one motif (it is hardly more than motif) half a dozen times. Notwithstanding its evocative Prologue, its iterated "unifying" symbols, and its turgid "Hegelian" dialectic of Act One, *The Mountains* is episodic to a fault. (*Welcome to Our City* and *Mannerhouse* share this crippling defect.) Still, we have reason to be grateful for Thomas Wolfe's having briefly, haltingly ventured into dramaturgy.

"*He was angry because he was poverty-stricken in symbols: his mind was caught in a net because he had no words to work with.*" The voice is Wolfe the novelist's, describing Eugene Gant in infancy.[76] Midway through his first novel, we encounter symbols, words, character, and action masterfully fused (as Eugene's classmate struggles with Schiller's play *Wilhelm Tell*):

"*The mountains,*" *observed John Dorsey, touched, in a happy moment, by the genius of the place,* "*have been the traditional seat of liberty.*"
Eugene turned his face toward the western ranges. He heard, far off, a whistle, a remote thunder on the rails.[77]

Out of an unpromising amalgam of Tom-Sam-Richard, this more confident Wolfe had forged Tom-Eugene; and his opposing central

75. *You Can't Go Home Again*, p. 145. The recurrence of the name "Weaver" (English) as "Webber" (German) is noteworthy.
76. *Look Homeward, Angel*, p. 37.
77. *Ibid.*, p. 319.

symbols of *The Mountains*, now superbly transmuted, anticipate the haunting final lines of *Look Homeward, Angel*:

... And he heard the whistle wail along the river.

Yet, as he stood for the last time by the angels of his father's porch, it seemed as if the Square already were far and lost; or, I should say, he was like a man who stands upon a hill above the town he has left, yet does not say, "The town is near," but turns his eyes upon the distant soaring ranges.

BIBLIOGRAPHY

DRAMATIC WRITINGS OF THOMAS WOLFE:
Concerning Honest Bob. Topical comedy. In *The [Carolina] Magazine,* XXXVII, v (May, 1920), 251–61.
Deferred Payment [The Convict's Theory]. In *The University [Carolina] Magazine,* XXXVI, iii (June, 1919), 139–53.
Gentlemen of the Press. Chicago: W. Targ, The Black Archer Press, 1942. Satiric sketch (27 pages) in dialogue form; not intended for dramatic production.
"The House at Belmont." Manuscript in Thomas Wolfe Collection, University of North Carolina Library.
"The House of Bateson." Manuscript fragments, 1922 (?). Harvard College Library MSS *46AM–7(19).
Mannerhouse. New York: Harper and Brothers, 1948 [produced by Yale Dramatic Association, May 5–7, 1949].
Mannerhouse. Manuscript drafts and typescripts of the play in its early stages, 1921–23. Harvard College Library MSS *46AM–7(6) to (8).
Mannerhouse. Typescripts, 1924–25. Harvard College Library MSS *46AM–7(9) and (10).
[Manuscript notes, drafts, manuscripts, and typescripts of one-act plays, 1918–20.] Harvard College Library MSS *46AM–7(15) to (18).
[Manuscript notes and drafts for plays, sketches, and essays, 1920–24.] Harvard College Library MSS *46AM–7(20) to (22).
The Mountains. A Play in One Act. Promptbook edition by Pat M. Ryan. San Luis Obispo, California, 1963 [as produced by the 47 Workshop of Harvard College, October 21 and 22, 1921, at Agassiz House Theatre, Cambridge, Massachusetts].
The Mountains. Promptbook of the one-act play. American Literature Collection, Beinecke Library, Yale University.
The Mountains. A Play in One Act. Typescript, 1921. Harvard Dramatic Club Library MS *M20; Harvard College Library MS Thr216 *68M86.
The Mountains. Manuscript drafts and typescripts of the one-act play, 1920–21. Harvard College Library MSS *46AM–7(1) to (4).
The Mountains. Typescript of the three-act and prologue version, 1922. Harvard College Library MS *46AM–7(5).
The Return of Buck Gavin. One-act play. In *Carolina Folk Plays, Second Series,* ed. Frederick H. Koch. New York: Henry Holt and Company, 1941. Pp. 31–44 [produced at the Chapel Hill High School Auditorium, March 14 and 15, 1919].
The Streets of Durham: or, Dirty Work at the Crossroads. Dramatic satire. In *The Carolina Tar Baby,* n.s. I, iii (November 18, 1919), 4, 5, 14.
"The Strikers." One-act play written at Chapel Hill. Harvard College Library MS *46AM–7(15).

The Third Night. One-act play. In *Carolina Folk Plays, First, Second, and Third Series,* ed. Frederick H. Koch. New York: Henry Holt and Company, 1941. Pp. 70–75 [produced at the Chapel Hill High School Auditorium, December 12 and 13, 1919].

Welcome to Our City. Play in 10 scenes. In *Esquire,* XLVIII (October, 1957), 57–83 [produced by the 47 Workshop of Harvard College, May 11, 1923].

Welcome to Our City. Three typescripts, 1925. Harvard College Library MSS *46AM–7(13) and (14).

Welcome to Our City. Manuscript notes and drafts, typescripts, casting notes, and set drawings, 1922–23. Harvard College Library MSS *46AM–7(11) and (12).

Welcome to Our City. Typescript, 1925 (?). Thomas Wolfe Collection, University of North Carolina Library.

SELECTED WRITINGS RELATING TO THOMAS WOLFE AS DRAMATIST:

Adams, Agatha Boyd. *Thomas Wolfe: Carolina Student.* Chapel Hill: University of North Carolina Library, 1950.

Baker, George Pierce. *Dramatic Technique.* Boston: Houghton-Mifflin, 1919.

Barber, Philip. "Tom Wolfe Writes a Play," *Harper's,* CCXVI (May, 1958), 71–76 [*Welcome to Our City*].

Benjamin, Paul L. "The Carolina Playmakers," *The Survey,* XLVIII (July 1, 1922), 436–40, 482.

Brown, John Mason. "The Four Georges: G. P. Baker at Work," *Theatre Arts Monthly,* XVII (July, 1933), 536–51 [reprinted in *Dramatis Personae* (New York: Viking Press, 1963), pp. 389–98].

———. "Thomas Wolfe When He Hoped to Write Plays," *New York Post,* September 21, 1938 [reprinted in *Dramatis Personae,* pp. 398–401].

Carpenter, Frederic I. *American Literature and the Dream.* New York: Philosophical Library, 1955 [*Mannerhouse*].

———. "The Autobiography of an Idea," *University of Kansas City Review,* XII (Spring, 1946), 179–87.

Daniels, Jonathan. *Tar Heels.* New York: Dodd, Mead, and Company, 1941.

Eaton, Walter Prichard. "Baker's Method of Making Playwrights," *The Bookman,* XLIX (June, 1919), 478–80.

———. "A Play by Thomas Wolfe," *New York Herald-Tribune Book Review,* January 30, 1949, p. 20 [*Mannerhouse*].

Fagin, N. Bryllion ."In Search of an American *Cherry Orchard,*" *Texas Quarterly,* I (Summer-Autumn, 1958), 132–41 [*Mannerhouse*].

Frenz, Horst. "A German Home for *Mannerhouse,*" *Theatre Arts,* XL (August, 1956), 62–63, 95.

———. "Thomas Wolfe als Dramatiker," *Die Neueren Sprachen,* IV (1956), 153–57.

Gibbs, Robert Coleman. "Thomas Wolfe's Four Years at Chapel Hill: A Study of Biographical Source Material." M.A. Thesis, University of North Carolina, 1958.

Henderson, Archibald. "Thomas Wolfe, Playmaker," *The Carolina Play-Book*, XVI, i (March-June, 1943), 29.

Holman, C. Hugh. *Thomas Wolfe*. Minneapolis: University of Minnesota Press, 1960.

Hutsell, James K. "As They Recall Thomas Wolfe," *Southern Packet*, IV (April, 1948), 4, 9–10.

Isaacs, Edith J. R. "The Carolina Playmakers: Their Contribution to American Art," *American Magazine of Art*, XXI (September, 1930), 506–13.

Johnson, Pamela Hansford. *Hungry Gulliver*. New York: Charles Scribner's Sons, 1948.

Kennedy, Richard S. "A Critical Biography of Thomas Wolfe to His Thirty-Fourth Year." Ph.D. Thesis, Harvard University, 1953.

——. "Thomas Wolfe at Harvard, 1920–1923," *Harvard Library Bulletin*, IV, ii (Spring, 1950), 172–90; iii (Summer, 1950), 304–19.

——. *The Window of Memory: The Literary Career of Thomas Wolfe*. Chapel Hill: University of North Carolina Press, 1962.

Kinkead, Cleves. "How the Work Is Done by Professor Baker's Dozen," Drama Section, *The New York Times*, September 15, 1915, p. 3.

Kinne, Wisner Payne. *George Pierce Baker and the American Theatre*. Cambridge, Mass.: Harvard University Press, 1954.

Koch, Frederick H. "Drama in the South," *The Carolina Play-book*, XIII, ii (June, 1940), 52–65.

——. "Folk-Play Making," *Carolina Folk Plays*. New York: Henry Holt and Company, 1922, pp. xi-xxix.

LaSalle, Claude William II. "Thomas Wolfe: The Dramatic Apprenticeship." Ph.D. thesis, University of Pennsylvania, 1964. [Copyright 1965.]

McElderry, Bruce R., Jr. *Thomas Wolfe*. New Haven: Twayne Publishers, 1964.

——. "Thomas Wolfe, Dramatist," *Modern Drama*, V (May, 1963), 1–11.

Nowell, Elizabeth. *Thomas Wolfe: A Biography*. New York: Doubleday and Company, 1960.

Rubin, Louis D., Jr. *Thomas Wolfe: The Weather of His Youth*. Baton Rouge: Louisiana State University Press, 1955.

Selden, Samuel, and Mary Tom Sphangos. *Frederick Henry Koch: Pioneer Playmaker*. Chapel Hill: University of North Carolina Library, 1954.

Stahr, Alden. "Thomas Wolfe of Chapel Hill," *The Carolina Magazine*, LXI (April 10, 1932), 1, 7.

Turnbull, Andrew. *Thomas Wolfe*. New York: Charles Scribner's Sons, 1968.

Walser, Richard. "A First Play by a Noted Novelist," *North Carolina Drama*. Richmond: Garrett & Massil, Inc., 1956, pp. 94–95.

Wolfe, Thomas. "The Beginnings of a Native American Drama Since 1890" (Outline for a Thesis), Spring, 1921. Harvard College Library MS *46AM–8(5).

——. *The Correspondence of Thomas Wolfe and Homer Andrew Watt*, eds. Oscar Cargill and Thomas Clark Pollock. New York: New York University Press, 1954.

——. "The Drammer," *The University* [*Carolina*] *Magazine*, XXXVI (April, 1919), 72–74 [satiric verse].

——. *The Letters of Thomas Wolfe*, ed. Elizabeth Nowell. New York: Charles Scribner's Sons, 1956.

——. "The Man Who Lives with His Idea," *The Carolina Play-Book*, XVI, i (March-June, 1943), 15–22.

——. *The Letters of Thomas Wolfe to His Mother*, eds. C. Hugh Holman and Sue Fields Ross. Chapel Hill: University of North Carolina Press, 1968.

——. *Thomas Wolfe's Purdue Speech "Writing and Living,"* eds. William Braswell and Leslie A. Field. West Lafayette, Ind.: Purdue University Studies, 1964.

——. "Tom Wolfe on the Drama," ed. Frank Kearns, *Carolina Quarterly*, XI (1960), 5–10 [Wolfe's text, "A Biographical Statement," pp. 9–10].

——. "Writing Is My Life: Letters of Thomas Wolfe," *The Atlantic Monthly*, CLXXVIII (December, 1946), 60–66; CLXXIX (January, 1947), 39–45; CLXXIX (February, 1947), 55–61 [letters to Mrs. J. M. Roberts].

DRAMATIZATIONS OF THOMAS WOLFE NOVELS:

Four dramatizations of Wolfe's novels have been staged: *The Web and the Rock*, by Lester Cohen (Spa Theatre, Saratoga Springs, New York, August, 1950); *Look Homeward, Angel*, by Ketti Frings (Ethel Barrymore Theatre, New York, November, 1957); *Of Time and the River*, by Paul Baker (Baylor University Theatre, Waco, Texas, April, 1954); and *Thirty-Seven Octobers* [from all the works], by C. Hugh Holman (The Playmakers Theatre, Chapel Hill, April, 1969).

THE MOUNTAINS

A PLAY IN ONE ACT

by Thomas Wolfe

CHARACTERS

> WEAVER, *a mountain doctor*
> RICHARD, *his son*
> LAURA, *his daughter*
> TOM WEAVER, *the doctor's brother*
> MAG WEAVER, *Tom's Wife*
> ROBERTS ⎱ *mountaineers*
> SAM ⎰

SCENE: *A Mountain District in the Western Part of North Carolina.*

TIME: *The Present; along toward sundown of a day in June.*

SETTING: *The living room in the home of Dr. Weaver, a substantial, comfortable country dwelling. So far as a room may have atmosphere, some subtle reflection of the personalities of fine but opposite people who have lived here, this room is rich in its mixture of strength and sweetness. There is a sober pensive tone almost of melancholy, but not of gloom. This is probably due to the dark walnut panellings and doors, the old oaken furniture with the marble-topped table in the center and the dark-brown papering of the walls which, on even so bright a day as this, shades and softens the light. It is along toward sundown on a day early in June, and the opening of the hearth at the left center has been closed with an iron grating. [Two rifles stand against wall up L. from hearth.] Brassheaded pokers and tongs and a shovel flank the hearth, leaning against the hooks that are driven for this purpose. There is an old-fashioned ornateness about this room which does not prove objectionable, maybe because its essential quality absorbs its small frivolities. The very hooks for the tongs, for instance, have ornate brass knobs and perched athwart the iron match safe on the mantel above is a very knowing looking iron sparrow, inviting the touch on his back that will make him dive like a shot into the box and bring up a match impaled on his long beak. There is a large wooden clock on the mantel and a tall vase at either end flaring out to a fluted rim and decorated with gilt flowers. At the left backstage is the entrance opening to a hall which runs through the house. Across this hall may be seen a sofa with a hat rack and a mirror above. The entrance to the porch is through this hall and a corner of the porch can be seen through the double windows which are at the center and right backstage. A low-hanging pine bough comes down before the window. Dr. Weaver's desk is at the right upstage; it is a high old walnut desk.*

Lower down right is a bookcase filled with heavy medical-looking volumes. There is a door opening to a closet at the left upstage and hanging over the mantel is the portrait of a woman, frail and extraordinarily beautiful, dressed in the manner of thirty years ago. The floor is carpeted with a fine old faded rug and the marble-topped table in the center is strewn with books and papers. Comfortable looking arm chairs are grouped around the table. Through the window at the back may be seen a stretch of green valley land and reaching across in the distance a panorama of great wooded mountains, spotted with the passing of clouds between them and the sun, and covered with a blue haze which deepens like a heavy veil on the most distant peaks. In the extreme background, and isolated from the other mountains, is a crag, a freak of nature's architecture, which at this distance resembles strikingly the profile of an old, hook-nosed, sardonically grinning man. The view could not be called "peaceful." It is mighty in its great repose and full of power and quiet depth.

Laura comes up through the hall and enters the room. She is a small, beautifully moulded girl of twenty-two with dark mobile features and a flashing crown of brown hair. She goes over to the table and absently re-arranges the books, moves restlessly to the window and looks out for a moment then returns to the hearth, where she stands for a moment gazing at the portrait. She drums nervously on the mantel with her fingers and returns to the table and seats herself there. She selects a book at random and thumbs the pages indifferently. Scarcely is she seated when Richard appears outside the window and enters the hall. He carries a stem of laurel in his hand which he tosses with his cap on the sofa. Richard is of medium height and slight figure. He moves with a swift, erect sureness that gives authority and dignity to his bearing. His face is thin, but its features are strong and finely drawn, his eyes are dark and brooding and set far back in his head, his movements are quick and nervous, and when he talks he uses his whole body. His speech may be slow and thoughtful, or it may be staccato in its rush, one word fairly snapping at the heels of another, the while he is running his hands in his pockets or jerking them out again with lightning-like rapidity. He is a talkative, imaginative young man, given to boomerang speculations which end where they start, too often, and return to plague their author. Restraint, compromise, or the path generally called "the middle way" are held in contempt and disdain by Richard. He would tell you that on the level of a principle there can be no compromise, he believes that there is no middle way,—he can visualize only two forces in life;—a Spirit that seeks truth and one that denies it. Life to him means a conflict between these two. This is dualism, if you like. Richard knows of only one way to absorb his negations; that is to forget them and conquer them,—or be conquered. He wants to be either a splendid success or an impressive failure, and he is bound to be one or the other; for one has only to look at this boy to know that he would fit a respectable mediocrity no better than a square peg a round hole. Older men would probably say that he is fine but foolish,—in short, an "idealist." He could take fire at an idea and burn with such a steady flame that it might consume him. He can visualize evil or good as forces in as intense and tangible a form as a mystic of the middle ages; this requires imagination, and its fusing spirit runs like a flame through all the processes of his inner life.

As a man of medicine and a scientist his possibilities are incalculable. Most of the classmates who have recently graduated from medical college with him will go out and be fine, honest gentlemen, and a credit to their profession,—steady, earnest and useful men. But from Richard you can expect something more than this. He will tell you that he can see God through a microscope and, without his telling you, you would know he can see beauty and unity in the vast things of Nature,—or perhaps, something malignant and evil there. He has the capacity for work and yet, time and again, the things his classmates sweated to know came to him in one blinding flash of light. As he grows older and wiser he will use this same quality on men, and much of the beauty and the tragedy and the mystery in the hearts of men will be revealed to his deeper insight, to thrill and exalt him. It has been his fate, and it will continue to be his lot to struggle with the Angel of Vision, but from that uneven contest may emerge, if nothing destructive happens, a spirit that can look serenely through the rags of the world about him and still see that which is real and eternal. If this seems too eulogistic we can only reply that it fails in adequately conveying the fineness of Richard.

He stands in the doorway a moment mopping his brown face with a handkerchief and dusting the trousers of his rough grey tweed. As he enters the room Laura rises to meet him and we see he is very little the taller; there is in him both an elusive fineness of bearing and mould that identifies them as brother and sister.

LAURA: Oh, you, Dick?

RICHARD: Hello. Is pa home yet?

LAURA [*rises*]: He went to Beetree early this morning to see Ben Weathers. (*She looks out of the window*). [*Turns to right*]. He ought to be here now. There's no telling, though, Pa keeps going from morning to night. A country doctor has a hard time, Dick.

RICHARD [*Dick to chair L.*]: I suppose I'll be initiated soon. [*1 step down stage.*]

LAURA: Yes. He has more than he can do. Pa is getting old, Dick. [*Two steps forward.*] Have you noticed? (*After a moment.*) [*Down to table R.*] But where have you been all day? I waited dinner an hour for you.

RICHARD: I visited my old friend.

LAURA: Who's that?

RICHARD: Bald Pate. (*He moves to the window and looks at the peak.*)[1]

LAURA: Doubletop's much prettier. (*Laura goes to window.*)

RICHARD: From here, you mean. (*Goes to window.*) Bald Pate is my only friend among them. The rest are a lot of sneaking

---

1. Eight typescript lines deleted following this speech and stage direction, promptbook p. 4 (bottom). Pages 5 and 7 (only) appear to be the retyped state of a heavily cut earlier script: text on each of these pages is approximately one-half normal page length, and *all* stage directions (Wolfe's and the stage manager's) are neatly and uniformly typed in.

hypocrites pretending to be soft and green and waiting a chance to grind you down. [*Comes down to chair R.*]

LAURA: You're the same as you always were, Dick—about the mountains. (*Turns to window.*)

RICHARD: They hem you in and hold you and never let you go.

LAURA: You've been away for eight years. (*As though to break conversation takes two steps away, sees picture.*)

RICHARD: And now I'm back. (*He walks over to the mantel, looks at the portrait fixedly a minute, and speaks without turning away*). When I was four or five years old I can remember—mother (*The word has a strange unused sound to him and he says it awkwardly but with reverence.*) sitting here by the hearth night after night rocking away with me in her arms. (*He turns swiftly* [*to L.*]) Laura, I know it was the eternal black fear of that waiting that killed her.

LAURA [*standing perfectly still*]: Waiting! What waiting?

RICHARD: Waiting for pa to come in out of the mountains. She never knew when they'd bring him in with a bullet through him.

LAURA: I have felt the same fear, Dick. [*Goes to Dick, close, arm on shoulder.*] There's never a day goes by but what I feel it. And now, well you have come back, so I suppose it will be twice as great.

RICHARD (*drawing his breath sharply*) [*Richard crosses to window, Laura to chair*]: Ah! They're still at it, are they?

LAURA: Of course. Do you think it will ever end as long as Uncle Tom is alive?[2] [*Richard turns.*] He's been in three times this last week to see pa and I'm afraid it means trouble again.

RICHARD: They're both getting old. I had hoped it would be over.

LAURA [*Laura goes to Dick at window.*] (*Almost with a sob*): Over! Dick, it will never be over until there are no more to fight and kill.

RICHARD: No! I suppose not. They'll go on shooting and killing each other as long as they last. And all because of a quarrel

---

2. One line ("He lives for nothing but that awful fight.") deleted here.

we had nothing to do with. [*Richard goes to desk.*] We don't even know how it started. I could understand anyone as wild and rough as Uncle Tom going on with it but how a man like pa can keep it up is beyond me.[3]

LAURA (*seriously*): Do you think we can *train* ourselves away from our people, Dick?

RICHARD (*emphatically*): Yes! In a certain sense—the proper one. I've been home only two days and I can already see just what the last eight years has meant to me.

LAURA: Is it best to change that way, Dick [*Goes to R.*], when you have to live here? (*Pause. Nervously turning it on herself.*) Look at me. [*Turns.*] I have good chances of being a nice old maid simply because—

RICHARD: Because a mountaineer wants a woman who can qualify as a packhorse when he marries.

LAURA: And I'm afraid I can't qualify. (*With a little laugh.*) At least I'm not swamped with offers. (To L. end of table.) Ever since Pa sent me off to St. Genevieve's, they all stay away—even the boys I've known all my life.

RICHARD: You're not their kind, Laura. [*Down to chair, right.*] It's right that they should keep their distance.

LAURA [*sits in chair L.*]: Perhaps—but it's awfully lonesome.

RICHARD [*goes to Laura's chair L. Pats her hand*]: Don't you fret! Life has something better in store for you, Laura [*Sits on arm of her chair.*], and somehow or other I'm going to get it.

LAURA (*smiling*): All the tourists think mountain life is quite romantic.

RICHARD: They see it from the train window.[4]

LAURA: I've been reading a book—

RICHARD [*seated on Laura's chair*] (*scornfully*): The books! Oh yes. But if you should read a thousand books which told you the mountains were wild and free [and] the mountain people lead wild adventurous lives, would you believe them?

LAURA (*wistfully*): I'd *like* to believe them, Dick.

RICHARD: But you know it's a lie. You read of beautiful

3. Two lines (Laura's) deleted here.
4. Seven lines (Laura, 1; Richard, 6) deleted here.

mountain girls, mountain-Europas running around on their small bare feet, with their golden hair flying in the wind. (*He laughs contemptuously*.) Laura, how many beautiful mountain girls have you seen?

LAURA (*truthfully*): There aren't many.

RICHARD: They are big, rawboned, awkward girls made thin and rough with hard work. They are married off before they're twenty and at twenty-five they are breeding droves of children. At thirty (*He rises with a quick movement of distaste [goes toward window]*.)—well, at thirty they are broken and old.

LAURA: I'm afraid that's so.

RICHARD [*turns to Laura*]: I passed by Tom Bryce's shanty on my way up Bald Pate. You know where the place is, dug in on the side of the hill (*She nods*.)[5]—stretched out below there in a level plain of rhododendron and laurel. And in front of Tom's door, some six or eight dirty little children were grubbing, so dirty and skinny and weazened that they looked like little monkeys! I looked at all that beauty on one hand and at all that filth and squalor on the other and then I looked up around me at these mountains standing there eternally to guard these people away from life.

LAURA [*Laura rises, goes to Richard at window, turns him to her*]:[6] Poor old Dick. It was hard on you to come back, wasn't it? But it was fine, too.

RICHARD: No. It wasn't either hard or fine. I couldn't do anything else. I've been gone eight years and there hasn't been a day of that time but what I could see these people back here, tired, gaunt creatures, fighting their pitiful little battle with the mountains which[7] shut them off from the ways of other men.

LAURA: It's not the ways of other men they need, Dick, so much as some more decent way of living their own lives.

RICHARD: It's the mountains, Laura, the mountains that use them up and kill them.

LAURA: Don't say that. I love the mountains, Dick. They are fine and beautiful.

5. Five short phrases and one stage direction deleted from the concluding portion of this speech.
6. Replaces original stage directions: "(*Patting his shoulders*.)"
7. Deletion of "hem them in and."

RICHARD: You've never felt their tyranny [*Laura turns away left.*]—except perhaps—(*He hesitates.*) in some . . .

LAURA (*Looking at him steadily*): Except that they've kept me away from—from people.

RICHARD (*flushing*): Well—yes.[8] When the people try to eke a living out of the ground, the mountains give up a *half* living—choosing to kill by inches.[9]

LAURA: Perhaps. But people don't leave them. There must be a reason for it. [*To table.*]

RICHARD: There is,[10] Laura. A man may leave the town or the farm or the sea, and stay away, but it isn't often he can leave the mountains. (*He turns to the window and is staring out at the peaks in the distance.*)

LAURA (*softly, taking an impulsive little step toward him*) [*goes toward him again*]: Is that why you came back, Dick?

RICHARD (*after a pause*) [*Richard turns a little toward L.*]: Maybe so, I can't exactly tell you why. God knows I hate those hills over there.

LAURA (*shocked*) [*Steps back*]: Oh, you don't mean that.

RICHARD: They stand over against me there as something evil, like the witches in *Macbeth*.

LAURA [*Laura crosses to chair L.*]: Your boyhood notions, Dick. You used to frighten me half to death when you talked like that. Heavens! What an imagination you had! [*Sits.*] I was afraid to step outside after dark for fear the mountains would[11] *gobble us up.*

RICHARD (*sadly*): They get a great many, Laura—people like Tom Bryce, slaving his life away on the side of a hill to keep food in the mouth of those six little wretches[12] and his snuff-dipping wife.[13] She was under forty when I left[14] but she had that stolid hopeless look then as if she were tired of living.

8. Four typescript lines deleted here.
9. Three lines (Laura, 2; Richard, 1) deleted here.
10. Deletion of "The mountains hold what is theirs."
11. Deletion of "get me. You said they were waiting to."
12. Replaces "wretched children."
13. Replaces "that poor snuff-dipping crone of a wife."
14. Deletion of "eight years ago."

LAURA (*softly*): She died while you were gone, Dick.

RICHARD (*with reverence*): Poor woman. What a life. [*Turns right, paces R. & L. back of table.*] (*With an outburst.*) There's the terrible story these brooding hills have to tell, a story of existence where people eat, sleep and die in one room foul with the[15] smell of dirty bodies, of haggard women lying—in such places giving birth to one child after another while the little unwashed, unkempt devils swarm around on the floor like so many flies. [*Finishes by chair R.*]

LAURA (*with a shiver*): I'd rather believe the books, Dick. You're too much of a realist.

RICHARD: It's the truth, Laura. [*Richard goes to left of table.*] And that is something most people hate to face. [*Pause.*]

LAURA (*presently*): I suppose you notice it more having lived in the city so long.

RICHARD: Yes.[16] For eight years now I've carried the picture with me of these miserable people beating their lives away against the side of a hill;[17] a picture that haunted and hurt. It brought me back and here I'll stay.[18] [*Returns, goes to window.*] I believe I have a job to do. I used to say to the mountains, "You can be beat and I'll do it some day."

LAURA: You're a dreamer, Dick, but I think you're fine. [*Laura rises, goes back towards window.*] I've wanted you back with all my heart—at times I thought I'd go crazy at the loneliness of it all. [*Richard moves towards her.*] I wanted the old days back when you would tease me, and yank my hair, or pull me up a hill behind you.

RICHARD [*Richard goes up to her, takes her outstretched hands behind table*] (*his eyes shining*): We'll do it again, Laura— go up the hill I mean. I reckon we're not too old for that.

LAURA: But there have been times, when I wasn't thinking of myself, that I hoped [*Laura draws away 2 steps, lower tone.*], I almost prayed you wouldn't come back.

15. Deletion of "stale."
16. Five typescript lines deleted here.
17. Deletion of "it was."
18. Deletion of "I feel I have a place here."

RICHARD (*startled*): What do you mean, Laura?

LAURA (*going up to him impulsively*) [*flings herself on him, clings to him*]: Dick, Dick, you're too fine a fellow to waste yourself up here.

RICHARD: I won't waste myself. I might have made more money by practicing in the city but I can do real work here. (*Enthusiastically.*) Why, Laura, I can do wonders. [*Laura draws away.*] Think of all these people—

LAURA: I don't mean money, Dick, If you only had a free hand to help these people you would do wonders. I'm sure of that.

RICHARD (*puzzled*): A free hand?

LAURA: The same thing happened to pa, that I'm afraid— [*Turns away ½ step.*] (*She stops.*)

RICHARD: Will happen to me? Is that what you mean? (*She nods. Richard continues with the utmost earnestness.*) I tell you I will never take part in it.[19] I think I'd sooner die. See what it has done to pa. Think of what he might have been, what he might have done up here if he hadn't lined up with one side. [*Richard steps forward.*]

LAURA: Pa's a good man, Dick. We'll never know a better [*Takes a step.*] But he couldn't go against his family. Don't you see it's hopeless? Why, Uncle Tom has looked forward to your coming back all this time. It has never occurred to him that you might be changed. He can't see anything else in life but a fight with the Gudgers. Every week he comes in and cleans and oils your rifle till it fairly shines. And when he puts it back in the closet he always says: "Just wait till Dick gets home, we'll show them a thing or two." That's what you've got to face, Dick.

RICHARD: All right, then. If things stand that way I'm ready to face them and to tell them I'll take no part in their game. And the sooner I get that settled the better. (*In passionate anger.*) Haven't they made it hard enough on you and me? [*Steps towards left.*] Won't my work up here be all the harder because everyone in the whole country is snarling at each other from two armed camps? Why, I believe the Gudger and Fitzpatrick people [*Down*

19. Deletion of "again."

between table and chair.] would rather die than ask help from pa. And he's the only doctor up here.

LAURA: But how can you do it? Don't you know what it means to belong to a mountain family, to (*Repeating with emphasis.*) *belong* to it?

RICHARD (*angrily*) [*crosses front of table to left front of chair*]: Family be damned. I won't commit murder—that's what it is—for all the families in the world. I've got my own life to lead.

LAURA [*L. down by chair*]: Are you sure it's your own?

RICHARD: Who do you think it belongs to?

LAURA [*comes further down, right of table*]: It ought to be yours, but is it?

RICHARD: It has to be.

LAURA: There are many things that stand between us all and the freedom we want for ourselves.

RICHARD [*Richard turns. Crosses to her right*]: What are you driving at, Laura? [*Pause.*] (*He looks at her hurt and surprised at her attitude.*) I had looked to you for support. You know what I have dreamed of doing here. Do you think me just a fool?

LAURA [*Laura goes to him*]: I wish there were more fools like you.

RICHARD: Why do you side against me, then?

LAURA (*gently*) [*looking up at him*]: I never have and I never will side against you, Dick. I—love you too much.

RICHARD (*quickly seizing her hands*): I know you do. But you mustn't lose heart, Laura. We are brave enough and strong enough to look them all in the face and refuse them.

LAURA (*clinging to him*) [*says into his shoulder*]: I'm afraid, Dick. I'm afraid for you. I hate to see you made unhappy and wretched. I hate to see your dreams broken. (*Head up.*) Dick, you'll give in, in the end. There's no way out of it. Pa had to and I know he was fine when he came back as you are. (*Loyally.*) He still is. (*Speaking rapidly and earnestly.*) Oh go, please go, Dick. (*Pushing him off.*) Go away from it all. If you don't, you are lost.

RICHARD: Lost! Run away now? Why, I've just begun to fight.

LAURA: Yes, yes—but you can't win.

RICHARD: But I can. (*After a pause.*) Has anything happened lately?

LAURA: Yes. Last week. Someone shot at cousin Joe Weaver. They don't know who it was.

RICHARD [*Richard turns, goes to end of table left*]: Was Joe hurt?

LAURA: No.

RICHARD: I suppose they're up in arms about it.

LAURA: I'm afraid it won't take much to start them again. I told you Uncle Tom had kept coming in to see pa this week.

RICHARD (*angrily*): I can't understand it. [*Quick turn to mantel and back.*] I never could. To think pa would allow himself to be drawn into it. I believe he hates the whole thing as much as I do. [*Turns back towards Laura.*]

LAURA: Don't blame him too soon, Dick.

RICHARD: If there's any reason for carrying on this fight except prejudice and stubbornness I've never—(*A man goes by the window. There are steps on the veranda. Laura looks warningly at Richard.*) [*Richard goes to fireplace left.*]

LAURA: Psh! Here he comes! [*Goes to open the door.*]

Dr. Weaver enters the hall. He deposits his little square satchel on the sofa and hangs his dusty felt hat on the rack. Dr. Weaver is a heavy, florid-faced man of medium height and slightly over fifty years old. He is smooth-shaven and his hair is short and grizzly gray. His face is seamed with heavy decisive lines which do not detract, however, from his genial, good-humored features. The total impression from the man is one of kindness linked to strength and character. He stands in the door knocking the dust from his baggy clothes and tramps heavily into the room. He greets Laura with a rough affectionate hug. [She takes his case.]

RICHARD (*affectionately*): Hello, pa.

WEAVER: Good evenin', son. (*Giving Laura another bearlike squeeze.*) What do you think of your sister, Dick? She's a grown-up lady, ain't she? [*They come into room.*]

RICHARD: And a mighty pretty one, too.

WEAVER [*looks up at picture*]: She gets more like her mother every day. I reckon I can't say no more than that. [*Brings her toward table C.*]

LAURA: I think both of you have said enough already. Are you hungry, pa?

WEAVER: I could eat a horse; got me any supper?

LAURA (*contritely*): I'm sorry. I lost track of time here talking to Dick. I'll have it in a hurry. (*She goes out.*)

WEAVER (*calling after*): Cut a few chunks off that side of ham I got from Tom Wilson. [*Goes L. to chair. Richard still at fireplace.*] Well, son, what have you done with yourself today? [*He has sunk heavily into a chair.*]

RICHARD: Oh, I climbed Bald Pate.

WEAVER: Climbed Bald Pate! How[20] I'd like to be young and spry again. I've been over every one of these hills from bonnet to bootstrap, you might say. (*Richard slaps Weaver on back.*) Son, reach into that desk and get me that box of cigars. (*Richard [goes to desk.] pulls down the lid of the desk and offers the box to his father, who selects a cigar. Richard starts to return the box.*) Go ahead and take one. I reckon you smoke behind my back. (*Richard selects a cigar a little sheepishly and puts the box back.*)

RICHARD [*puts box back. Stays right*]: You see—I don't think you've ever seen me smoke before.

WEAVER: I hope not. You were just a shoot of a seventeen-year-old boy when I sent you off. (*He has lighted his cigar and sinks back in his chair [left] a little wearily.*)

RICHARD [*Pause. Stands at desk*]: Tired, pa? (*Weaver nods.*) Had a hard day, I guess?

WEAVER: I came close to drivin' the legs off the mare. I went to Beetree to see Ben Weathers.

RICHARD: What's wrong with Ben? (*Sits right of table.*)

WEAVER (*wearily*): The same old story. He got into a fight last night with a fellow in Marion and they carved each other up a bit. Both had licker in 'em, I reckon. But, pshaw! You can't kill 'em. Like as not they'll be at it again next week. (*Good humoredly.*) If he does I'll send you to see him.

20. Deletion of "Oh" preceding "How."

RICHARD: Well, I'm ready to start any time now.

WEAVER: Take your time, son. You'll have enough to do once you get started. I don't know how it's going to feel with another medico up here. I've been the only one for thirty years. But I'm getting old, Dick. It won't be many years before you'll have the reins in your own hands. I reckon you came along about the right time.

RICHARD: They'll hate to lose you, pa. These people think a lot of you.

WEAVER: Do they? I wonder, now. Some of them, maybe. Not all, Dick. Not all. There are people here, son, who would lay down and die before they'd ask me in to help them. Our friends, the Gudgers, for instance.

RICHARD: Haven't they ever called you in?

WEAVER: Nary a time.

RICHARD: But surely they needed you.

WEAVER: They've needed me often enough and no mistake. But they're all stubborn as mules. Only last year Bob Gudger—he's the cousin of Clem down here at the store—got down with pneumonia.

RICHARD: And they never called you in! [*Pause.*] How'd he get along?

WEAVER (*grimly*): He died. (*In a tone of deep bitterness, but with unmistakable regret also.*) Served them right, the fools. I've never refused to go anywhere I was needed day or night for thirty years. They can't blame me. I'd have gone if they had asked me. (*He looks searchingly at Richard.*)

RICHARD (*evasively*): They should have called you in, of course.

WEAVER: Of course they should have. What fools they are! (*Laughing suddenly.*) You'll meet all kinds up here. I set a fellow's leg last week who thought he was a bird.

RICHARD: A bird!

WEAVER: He was a mountaineer from way back yonder in Madison. The poor fellow saw an airplane fly for the first time at the fair in Morganton. He went home and took a pair of eagle's wings—given him by his daddy, he says, and somehow or other he got them hitched on to his shoulders. He climbed a tree and stepped off.

RICHARD (*laughing in spite of himself*): It's a wonder he didn't kill himself. Lucky he didn't try a cliff.[21]

WEAVER: That mountaineer can't understand yet what went wrong.

RICHARD [*rising*]: Poor, ignorant devils!

WEAVER (*very gravely*): They're your own people, son. You came from that stock.

RICHARD [*stepping to table*]: Yes, but of course it's different with us. [*Sits on table front, left.*] Education makes a lot of difference and [*Pause.*] —we're just not like Uncle Tom and his people any more.

WEAVER [*brings chair close to table*]: Dick, mountain people live a whole lot closer together than any other people I've known. And all the education in the world can't change the fact of kith and kin. It took me nearly a life time to learn[22] that. And I want you to learn it now.

RICHARD: What do you mean by "closer together"?

WEAVER: Toward each other. The family tie binds us all together; a man can't get away from his family; he gets to the point he doesn't want to.

RICHARD: Why—he shouldn't want to, should he? [*Weaver turns aside, eyes drop.*] (*He looks at his father startled* [*then looks away*].) Oh!

WEAVER (*with a faint smile*): I don't suppose he should. But when we're young and full of fine ideas we want to be what we call—free. Later on—(*He stops.*)

RICHARD: Do fine ideas have to go by the boards later on!

WEAVER: Some do, Dick.

RICHARD: I'd hate to believe it.

WEAVER: I wouldn't want you to, son. It's not all true either. There's always honey mixed with the gall and wormwood. If I'd stayed in the city I might have had a fat practice built up. And from the money side of it practicing up here is a sorry business. But I

21. Five typescript lines (Richard, 4; Weaver, 1) deleted here.
22. The words "it now" are crossed out here.

wanted to get back. I don't think I could have stayed away. Sometimes I'm sorry I came. But there are times when it all seems worth while. After all, I'm the only doctor up here, or was, until you came. What would they have done without me?

RICHARD: It keeps you busy, though.

WEAVER: There's hardly a minute I can call my own. I have so much to do that I reckon I've become a sort of crude carpenter. I often do things you and the young squirts you graduated with would hoot at. Do you remember Jim Stafford's little boy?

RICHARD: Yes! He ought to be about twelve now.

WEAVER: He's only ten. I was driving by Jim's house two weeks ago and he came running out and called me in. The boy had swallowed a chicken bone and it lodged in his throat cutting off his wind entirely. He was blue in the face when I got there. He couldn't have lasted much longer. I didn't have anything with me but my pill case.

RICHARD: What did you do?

WEAVER (*after some hesitation*): I used my pocket knife, Dick.

RICHARD: Good God! [*Rises, right of table.*]

WEAVER (*apologetically*): I don't suppose it sounds very nice. But I saved the boy's life if I do say it myself. (*With some pride.*) And I made a clean job of it, too. A small incision under the jaw that's going to heal with hardly a scar. [*Richard turns slowly right around table.*]

RICHARD: And Laura never said a word about it!

WEAVER: I never told her. (*Warningly.*) Don't say anything about it to her. Laura's like your mother, Dick—just as soft-hearted as can be. It would only worry her. [*Richard to L. of table.*] Besides, it's all in the day's work, as the saying is.

RICHARD: Why, it's as fine a thing as I ever heard of. See here! [*Sits on left end of table.*] I'm going to write it up for the medical journal tonight. You'll be famous for that.

WEAVER: Oh, no you don't. I don't care to be advertised for doing my duty. [*Tom gets ready for knock.*] (*There is a knocking at the door.*) I'll see who it is.

[*Richard rises, goes toward door.*] *Weaver goes into the hall and opens the door. He is heard greeting his visitor outside: "How-dy, Tom. Come in." "Howdy, Dick, how're you-all. Jest come in fer a minute. Heard that young un of yourn's back agin." They enter the room. Richard rises to greet his uncle, Tom Weaver, a typical mountaineer—a man of forty-five, but apparently older. He is lean to gauntness, his tall bony frame is stooped, his long arms hang dangling to his knees. His skin has the tanned leather finish that comes from exposure to all kinds of weather, his eyes are beady and glittering and his movements quick and nervous. He is dressed in a rough suit of corduroy, and his faded shirt is collar-less. Thin wisps of greyish hair stick through the crown of his tat-tered felt hat. The physical contrast between Tom and his brother, however, hardly begins to indicate the unmeasured chasm in edu-cation and training; yet they seem to recognize no difference here, they are natural, unaffected and entirely at their ease with each other.*

WEAVER: Dick, here's your Uncle Tom come to see you.

RICHARD: Hello, Uncle Tom.

TOM WEAVER: Howdy, Dicky. (*They shake hands awkward-ly. Tom surveys him critically for a moment.*) By God, Dick, he's run up like a weed. It don't seem no time since I rode him on my knee. I gave him his first chew of terbaccer when he wasn't ten year old.

RICHARD (*laughingly*): My first and last, Uncle Tom.

TOM WEAVER: Start 'em early, I say. You'll cure 'em, kill 'em, or larn 'em. (*To Weaver.*) Why, I had this feller lookin' down the barrel of a gun when he wasn't hardly able to lift hit an' when he reached sixteen he was showin' me stunts I never thought of. Slickest shot with a gun I ever seen, Dick, not meaning to give him the big-head. He could shave ye with one shot an' come back an' give ye a hair-cut with t'other. [*All laugh.*]

RICHARD: I had a good teacher, Uncle Tom.

TOM WEAVER: Well, ye'll be gettin' a chance to show ye ain't forgotten how. I was tellin' yore pa t'other day—

WEAVER (*quickly and with a warning look*): Tom, you've got to stay for a bite of supper now you're here. Laura's nearly ready with it now.

TOM WEAVER (*dubiously*): I dunno. I reckon I ought to be gettin' back an' do my chores. The ole gal's waitin' on me outside now.

WEAVER: Is Mag with you?

TOM WEAVER: Yeh! I left her out with the mules. She said she reckoned she wouldn't come in.

WEAVER: Bring her right in.

TOM WEAVER: Don't you reckon hit'll put you out? [*Richard looks out window.*]

WEAVER: Not a bit. There's plenty of room for all of us. I'll have Laura set two extra places.

TOM WEAVER (*going to the window and calling out*): Hey, gal, tie them mules up an' come on in. We're stayin' for supper.

A WOMAN'S VOICE (*outside—shrill, cracked and strident*): Law me! I hain't fit to be seen in company. I'll be right in.

TOM WEAVER ([*stops by window right*] *with a chuckle*): It ain't often she gits the chance to eat somebody else's cookin'.

A woman enters. She is a hard unlovely looking creature, her sallow skin is stretched tightly over her sharp, bony face, her wispy hair has been pulled back painfully and fastened in a knot behind; from the corner of her mouth protrudes a small stick; her mouth is discolored with snuff at the edges. She is dressed in gingham which fits her shapeless body tightly; she moves awkwardly and is deeply embarrassed by the presence of so much unaccustomed luxury in her surroundings. Richard steps quickly to her and takes her hand.

RICHARD: Hello, Aunt Mag.

MAG: Well, now! Haint he growed up, though! You'd be a right pert catch fer any gal, Dick.

RICHARD (*laughing*): Well, I haven't thought of anything like that, Aunt Mag.

MAG (*approvingly*): That's right, son. Ye'd better stay shet of it. I never knowed no better.

TOM WEAVER: You're gettin' mighty set-up an' sassy, ain't you? Where'd you be now if I hadn't come along an' took ye? (*Cackling shrilly.*) First time I ever seen her she was hoein' potaters in her daddy's patch.

MAG (*laconically* [*Mag crosses to Tom*]): Yeh! I'm still hoein' 'em in yourn.

WEAVER (*with a chuckle*): She hit you that time, Tom. Make yourselves at home. I'm going back to wash up.

MAG: Where's Laurie?

WEAVER: She's back there fixing supper.

MAG [*crosses back*]: I'll go on back an' help her. I reckon Tom'll want to talk to Dick. [*Goes out.*]

She goes out with Weaver. Weaver is heard down the hall: "Your Uncle Tom and Aunt Mag are here to supper, Laura." Tom selects a chair and sits down looking at Richard appraisingly all the time. The silence between the two becomes strained and awkward, Richard trying desperately to find something to say, Tom chewing a wad of tobacco vigorously and never removing his gaze from Richard. [They stand silent; then Tom goes to fireplace, spits.]

RICHARD (*awkwardly*): I hope you've been well, Uncle Tom?

TOM WEAVER: Tolable, Dick, jest tolable.

RICHARD: And how is—your wife?

TOM WEAVER (*staring*): Who?

RICHARD (*confused*): Oh—Aunt Mag, I mean.

TOM WEAVER (*spitting*): Oh, the ole woman. Pshaw, Dick [*Sits in chair L.*], that's the sorriest critter I ever clapped eyes on. She ain't wurth her snuff, no she ain't. I'd as lief have no help at all as the kind of help she's been givin' me. She's ailin' an' complainin' all the time of fust one thing, the t'other. Hit's been her back hyeh lately but if hit ain't her back hit's somethin' else.

RICHARD: I'm very sorry to hear it. ([*Pause,*] *looking at Tom intently.*) Perhaps she's worked too hard, Uncle Tom.

TOM WEAVER: Work! She don't know nothin' about hit! What does a woman know about work, Dick? Of course they piddle aroun' the house a little an' cook an' wash some—

RICHARD [*stands, hands in pockets*]: And raise a family and sew and iron and do a few other things but after all they don't know much about work, do they? [*Richard sits right.*]

TOM WEAVER (*taking him quite seriously*): No. Nothin' to speak of. They lay aroun' eatin' you out of house an' home while you grub away on the farm tryin' to git things to grow atween the rocks. That's work! (*Plaintively*.) But the ole gal's gittin' ole, I reckon. So'm I. An' we ain't got no call to be.

RICHARD (*cheerfully*): Go on, Uncle Tom. You talk like you're an old man.

TOM WEAVER (*earnestly*): I am, Dick. I am.

RICHARD: Why, you can't be over forty-five and your—Aunt Mag's not forty, I bet.

TOM WEAVER: She's goin' on forty-one. But it ain't the number o' years ye live, son, that makes ye ole. Hit ain't "how long" but "how much." So we're gittin' ole, Dick, jest the same. (*With something like real sympathy*.) Pore ole gal, she *has* had a mighty hard time of hit.

RICHARD: You've had a large family to support, Uncle Tom.

TOM WEAVER: Yeh! A man oughter know better than to have a whole flock of young 'uns 'less'n he's able to do hit. I got a stand of land in the cove, ye know, but, law, hit ain't wuth shucks. Last spring the rains come an' never let up fer two weeks steady. All my young cawn was beat right into the ground. I guess all the water on Craggy drained right into my back yard. That cussed mountain causes half my trouble, son. Two years ago a flood came an' in a week the whole side of a hill started slidin' down on my house, slow an' easy, a few foot a day.

RICHARD: A landslide, eh?

TOM WEAVER: Yeh! That's what they call hit. I stopped hit but my crop went plumb to hell while the boys an' I were drivin' logs in front of the bank behind our house.

RICHARD [*Richard gets up, looks towards window*] (*roughly*): Pah! Do you think you'll stop a mountain by driving a few wooden sticks in the ground?[23] [*Richard turns to Tom.*]

TOM WEAVER: No. Hit'll git me some day, creepin' down on me a few foot a year. Son, I've gone out into my back yard o'nights when no one was lookin' an' cussed that damn mountain with every dirty name I could think of. I've tried my best to make a livin' fer thirty year an' the damned mountain seems to have a hand in spilin' my crop every time. Ye'd better be glad, son, ye don't have t' make

---

23. Two lines of stage directions deleted here.

yore livin' farmin'. I don't know nothin' else so I got to. I never seemed t' be able t' git away from up heah.

RICHARD [*at window*]: Haven't you ever been out of the mountains, Uncle Tom?

TOM WEAVER: Oh, I've been to Hick'ry a few times peddlin' melons, but pshaw, I couldn't stay away long. I wanted t' git back. Gawd knows why.

RICHARD: I know.

TOM WEAVER: Yore pa was different. He allus was a restless youngun an' wanted t' git away. He had a mind to doctorin' as fer back as I kin remember so he worked in ole man Tom Winthrop's hardware store fer $15.00 a month, an' read books at night 'til he was able t' git away.

RICHARD (*with deep admiration* [*crosses to back of table*]): That was fine. It took nerve to do that.

TOM WEAVER: Yore pa allus did have a lot of git-up-an-go to him, Dick. I never knowed how he made out while he was gone but one day he turned up bringin' the purtiest gal back from the city I ever clapped eye on.

RICHARD: That was my mother. (*Walks over to the hearth and looks at the picture. His back is to Tom. Tom looks at picture also.*)

TOM WEAVER: You don't remember her much, I reckon. Son, she was a fine woman. Quiet an' pale-like but as nice an' accomodatin' a gal as you ever see.

RICHARD [*turning to Tom*]: Tell me, Uncle Tom, do you think my mother liked it up here in the mountains? [*Richard stands by Tom's chair back.*] That is, did you ever hear her say anything—

TOM WEAVER: Well now, Dick, I can't rightly say as to that. All I know is yore ma worried right smart over yore pa.

RICHARD: Worried? Was it on account of that—

TOM WEAVER: Count o' the trouble with the Gudgers. Yes. You see he hadn't tol' her nothin' 'bout hit when he come back an' when she found out she made him promise he wouldn't have nothin' to do with hit. He tol' her he wouldn't. (*Chuckling.*) Yore pa had a lot o' queer notions when he fust come back, Dick.

RICHARD: Oh, he did. I suppose he soon lost them, did he?

TOM WEAVER: Oh, sure, when the time come. When he come back he said he wouldn't have nothin' t' do with hit, said he was back heah—(*Scratching his head.*)—said he was back heah "to cure an' not to kill," them was his very words.

RICHARD (*in a low, quiet voice*): Ah! He said that, did he? (*Speaking now with a trace of hard sarcasm in his voice which Tom doesn't notice.*) But you brought him around, Uncle Tom, didn't you?

TOM WEAVER: No-o, I can't say as we did anything, Dick. We jest let things slide along fer we knew when the time come yore pa was comin' with us. So one night shootin' broke out an' we come fer yore pa. He was settin' heah in this very room with yore ma.

RICHARD: Did he go with you?

TOM WEAVER: There wan't nothin' else to do. A man ain't goin' agin his family, is he? Besides, shootin' Gudgers comes more nachrul than shootin' squirrels to a Weaver. Hit's jest like yore pa tol' yore ma afore he left her that night. I'll never fergit hit. She hadn't said nothin' an' he kinder lifted his hands an' said, "Blood's[24] thicker'n water, Effie."

RICHARD [*down in front of Tom by fireplace*]: Uncle Tom, just what is it all about? What do we expect to get out of it? What are we fighting for?

TOM WEAVER (*grimly*): We're fightin' fer our lives, son.

RICHARD: Yes, but why? How did this thing ever start? [*Richard at side of Tom's chair.*] You've never told me. Pa never has.

TOM WEAVER: Oh, hit started way back thar afore you was born. Ole Man Jud Fitzpatrick had a passel of mountain land next to yore Grandaddy Weaver's t'other side o' Doubletop.

RICHARD [*a step away, back*]: Mountain land, you say.

TOM WEAVER: Yeah! They never did git hit cleared up where one line started an' t'other begun.

RICHARD: A dispute over a boundary line! [*Richard goes to window.*] (*Muttering.*) Mountain land. I might've known! [*Back to audience.*]

TOM WEAVER [*Richard turns and listens.*]: One day ole man Fitzpatrick come on yore Grandaddy fencin' his land an' he said:

24. Promptbook spelling: "blodd's."

"Who gave ye leave to fence my land?" Yore Grandaddy said: "Who said hit was yore land?" Ole man Fitzpatrick yells: "I say so, by God." "You don't need to git so hot about hit," yore Grandaddy says. "Thar ain't no call to go gittin' on yore head 'bout hit." Ole man Fitzpatrick goes off but he comes back in 'bout an' hour with a gun. He don't come close but he yells, "We'll see now if ye don't git off, damn ye!" an' he shoots at yore Grandaddy.

RICHARD: And he killed him?

TOM WEAVER (*with satisfaction*): No, damn him, he didn't. Yore Grandaddy laid fer him an' shot him two weeks after he was comin' from meetin'. (*Spits.*) Kill him deader'n a nail.

RICHARD: So that was it? Forty years of it! Where will it end, Uncle Tom? [*Comes down right of table.*]

TOM WEAVER [*Tom rises suddenly, crosses front of table to Richard's right*]: End! End! Thar ain't goin' to be no end, son, 'til we git all that gang or they git us.

RICHARD: And so, I suppose we'll go on shooting and killing each other until there are no more to shoot and kill. What are we gaining by it, Uncle Tom? [*Richard to front. Face each other.*] We're not settling anything. There's a law for killing.

TOM WEAVER (*savagely*): Yeh! An' I mean to take hit in my own hands. (*Turning suddenly on Richard.*) [*Richard steps back to chair.*] You look heah, Dick: I don't know what new notions you got in yore head since you been gone. But don't you let 'em interfere with business. Yore business when the time comes will be totin' a gun along with yore pa. Don't you fergit that, Dick. (*He goes to* [*wall up from fireplace and*]²⁵ *takes a highly polished rifle.* [*Richard watches a moment.*] *He handles it with loving care and the expression of his harsh, seamed face becomes gentle for a moment and he smiles.*) Pshaw, Dick! You ought to be proud to tote sech a gun. Look how purty I kep' it fer ye. All slick an' shiny an' ready fer business. (*Richard snatches the gun impulsively and examines it with ill-concealed eagerness.*) [*Tom comes down C. back of table.*]

RICHARD: Here! Let me have it. Been so long since I— (*He sights the rifle with a swift sure movement.*) It's light as a feather! Easy to handle as— (*He notices Tom's sardonic grin and releases*

25. Replaces "the closet."

the rifle in deep disgust.) Here! Take the damn thing! I don't want to ever see it again.

TOM WEAVER (*ironically*): Yeh! I seen how you fought shy of hit. (*He digs Richard in the ribs with a dry cackle.*) You'll do, Dick, you'll do.

RICHARD [*Richard turns on Tom*] (*angrily*): What? — Ah! [*He flings himself in chair—right of table.*]

TOM WEAVER [*sets gun down*] (*coming up to him and speaking very earnestly*): Son, I'm a broken down ole man but as long as I can tote a gun an' see to shoot one I'm ready to fight a Gudger. Yore pa an' I have waited fer ye, Dick, an' ye ain't goin' back on us now. Yore pa's gittin' ole, Dick, an' yore young an' stout as a mule. [*Tom bends over Richard's chair.*] You're a *Weaver*, Dick. Don't ye know what that means? Thar ain't nothin' else ye can do but go with yore tribe.

RICHARD (*rising furiously*): There's not? Well, we'll see, Uncle Tom. We'll just see about that.

TOM WEAVER (*with a tolerant smile*): Go on with the fireworks, son. You'll tone down when the time comes. You're yore daddy over again an' I know how he was. [*Puts gun back by hearth.*]

There is a knocking at the door. Richard starts to answer it but Laura passes by in the hall. She pauses a moment.

LAURA: Supper's ready, you folks. I'll see who's here.

She opens the door and ushers in a mountaineer, a man of thirty-five, evidently in a suppressed but highly keyed state of excitement. He shuffles in awkwardly, looks apprehensively at Richard and Tom, snatches his hat off suddenly and stands twisting it in his hands.

THE MAN [*anxiously*]: Good evenin', Miss Laura. I come to see yore pa. Is he in?

LAURA: Yes. I'll get him for you. Have a seat.

She goes out .Tom has been looking suspiciously at the visitor all the time and now half bustles up to him.

TOM WEAVER: Ain't ye one of them Roberts?

THE MAN (*half defiantly*): Ed Roberts my name.

TOM WEAVER (*contemptuously*): Hah! I knowed hit! What air ye doin' hyeh?

At this point Weaver enters, the man turns to him swiftly and speaks to him rapidly, earnestly, and with a note of pleading in his voice.

THE MAN: Doc, I come to ask ye to go out to my place with me. My leetle gal's been took with a cold an' she's been gaspin' since mornin' like she couldn't git her breath.

WEAVER: Where do you live?

THE MAN: Out on Beaverdam. I got a team hyeh, I'm all ready to go. (*Weaver starts for desk.*)

TOM WEAVER [*Tom at chair L.*] (*interjecting roughly*): D'ye know who this feller is, Dick? His name is Roberts; he's a cousin of Clem Gudger's.

RICHARD [*1 step forward*] (*excitedly*): It doesn't make any difference who he is. One of us ought to go with him.

[*Weaver walks over to desk—his back to Roberts.*]

THE MAN (*pleading earnestly to Weaver*): Doc, ye ain't goin' to throw me down count o' that, air ye? I ain't never had nothing to do with Clem Gudger nor his crowd. I ain't never harmed ye, Doc. I swear I ain't. [*Roberts crosses to desk.*] The ole woman's nigh crazy 'bout the gal, Doc. [*Weaver at desk.*] If I come back without ye I don't know what she'd do.

RICHARD (*in great excitement, breaking in*) [*comes down, crosses to Weaver*]: Pa! Let me go with him. I can—

WEAVER (*his pride touched into a moment's anger*): It's all right. I'm still able to tend to my own patients. (*He writes rapidly on the top of his desk.*) Here, Roberts [*Roberts crosses quickly to him.*], take this prescription down to Joe Wetherby's. Go to his house, the store's closed. Come back here as quick as you've got it filled. Make it quick, now, do you hear?

The Man snatches the prescription and goes out quickly. The door closes and his heavy boots may be heard clattering down the steps. There is absolute silence for a moment while Tom looks with amazement[26] at his brother.

---

26. Deletion of "apparent" before "amazement."

TOM WEAVER [*Tom crosses to front of table L.*]: You don't aim to go out thar with that feller, do ye?

WEAVER (*firmly*): I do.

TOM WEAVER: Didn't I tell ye he's Clem Gudger's cousin?

WEAVER: I'd go if it was Clem Gudger himself, Tom.

RICHARD [*Richard steps forward right*] (*with enthusiasm*): That's right, pa.

TOM WEAVER (*in deep disgust*): Hell! This beats all I ever heerd of.

WEAVER [*crosses to Tom*] (*slapping him affectionately on the back*): You mustn't take these things so seriously, Tom. I'm a doctor and I can't draw the line on a man because his family isn't agreeable to me.

TOM WEAVER: All the same we've got to stick together. We can't let it go gittin' 'round that we're hobnobbin' with any o' that crowd.

WEAVER: Pshaw! Don't make a mountain out of a mole hill, Tom. Think of the man's little girl. You can't let a child suffer. She might have pneumonia from the way he talked. (*There are sounds of footsteps on the steps outside.*) He's getting back mighty quick. (*A knocking at the door.*) Must be somebody else. (*He opens the door. A man, breathless from running, and greatly agitated, runs in.*)

WEAVER: What is it, Sam? (*Noting his agitation and speaking sharply.*) What's the matter, Sam?

SAM: Where's Tom? Is he here?

WEAVER (*jerking his head*): Inside. Come on in. (*Sam comes in quickly.*)

SAM [*Sam comes back of table C.*]: Clem Gudger killed Joe 'while ago.

TOM WEAVER (*leaping forward*) [*to L. of table*]: What! Where was he?

SAM: Joe went into Clem's store and tol' him he was the one who shot at him last week. Clem had been drinkin' an' he said: "No, damn ye, but I'll git ye now." So he pulled a gun from under his counter an' shot him.

TOM WEAVER (*turning passionately to Weaver and speaking in a voice choked with rage*) [*Sam moves to R. of table. Richard listens deeply agitated.*]: What did I tell ye? I knowed it was comin'. I've seen 'em with their heads together talkin'—all of 'em as quiet as rats when ye walked by 'em, an' I knowed hit was comin'. Now, damn 'em, we'll have it out. (*To Sam.*) Where air they now?

SAM: Clem an' two of the Fitzpatrick boys air down in the store with the doors locked. They're waiting on ye to come, I reckon. (*Mag and Laura enter.* [*Laura crosses to "Paw" quickly.*])

MAG: What is hit, Tom? (*Quickly.*) Has thar been shootin' agin?

TOM WEAVER [*at door*]: Joe Weaver's been killed. I was jest goin' t' git the boys. You stay here with Laurie, Mag. [*Turning to Weaver.*] By drivin' hard I can git back in four hours. Can you an' Dick drive over to Beaverdam an' get Cousin Joe and Bob Blackwell?

WEAVER (*slowly*): Why—I reckon, Tom.

TOM WEAVER: We'll have to hurry to do it in four hours. Sam you come along with me. (*He starts to go.*)

MAG [*Mag stopping him*]: Oh, Lord, I knowed hit was comin' agin. An' now ye'll go out thar, Tom, an' like as not git shot.

TOM WEAVER: You close yore trap, Mag. I ain't got no time to go foolin' with you.

MAG: No, you hain't never had no time to think of me. What's to become of me, Tom? A lot you care an' I've slaved fer ye nigh onto twenty-five year.

TOM WEAVER [*pushes her aside to L.*] (*roughly*): You stay like I tol' you with Laurie. I'll come an' git you as soon as it's over.

MAG: More'n likely they'll bring ye in with a bullet in you.

TOM WEAVER (*quickly*): Come on, Sam. I'll be expectin' ye back, Dick. (*He goes out with Sam.*)

WEAVER (*quietly after a moment to Richard*): I'll go get the buggy out. Meet me out front. [*Starts for door.*]

RICHARD (*in a low voice*): I'm not going with you. I'll go with Roberts when he comes back.

WEAVER [*stops, turns a few steps towards Richard*] (*firmly*): No, you'll come with me, Dick. There's nothing else you can do. (*Roberts comes in quickly.*)

ROBERTS [*coming to Weaver*]: Well, I'm ready, Doc. I got the medicine an' I reckon we better not lose no more time.

WEAVER (*after some hesitation*): I'm sorry, Roberts, but I can't go with you now.

ROBERTS: What's that? Aw—Doc, ye can't mean it. Why, ye jest tol' me ye'd go with me.

WEAVER: I know, but something has happened since then that makes it impossible. (*Roberts [takes steps]*[27] *hopefully to Richard.*)

RICHARD: Yes, Roberts, I'll go with you. (*He starts to go, but his father stops him.*) [*Roberts crosses to Richard.*]

WEAVER: Just a minute, Dick. I have something to say to you. (*Turning to Roberts.*) Roberts, go outside and wait. If my son can go with you he'll be out very soon.

ROBERTS (*with a menace in his voice*): All right, Doc Weaver, but let me tell ye somethin'. If anything happens to my leetle gal because ye won't go with me I'll git ye if I have to hunt ye the rest of my life. [*Comes close to Weaver.*]

WEAVER: That talk doesn't do you any good, Roberts. Now, go on out.

ROBERTS (*doggedly*): I ain't goin' to be throwed over like this. (*He goes out but turns for a moment at the door and speaks in a trembling voice.*) I ain't never harmed ye, Doc, but so help me Gawd, if anything happens— (*He goes out.*)

RICHARD (*impatiently*): Go on and say what you have to say, I'm going with him!

WEAVER: You're coming with me, Dick. It's your family that needs you tonight, my boy. And that's a call we can't resist. [*Puts hand on Richard's shoulder.*] Every day, every year of your life up here, you'll feel the tug of that call. If you despise it now you'll regret it all the days of your life.[28]

RICHARD (*stubbornly*): You can't make me go.

27. Replaces "turns."
28. Deletion of two lines (Weaver's) here.

WEAVER: I won't try. But you'll come, Dick. [*Richard moves to R.*] Oh, yes, you will. You think you can get away, Dick, if you have the schooling. I know, for I've been through the same mill. But you can't. You can't desert us all that way.

RICHARD (*desperately* [*turning on him*]): You're asking me to do a hideous thing. Don't you see, it's a test, a test when these two things come together this way and I won't give in. There's a bigger struggle than you and I have any idea of going on out there somewhere tonight and I'm going to line myself up on the right side. (*In a clear voice.*) Do you hear me? [*Crosses to door.*] I'm going with Roberts. [*He starts toward the door.*]

LAURA [*springing forward, stops him*] (*with a sharp cry*): Dick! Stop!

RICHARD: What! You? (*Brokenly.*) Oh, Laura, I thought you were with me. [*Throws Laura off.*]

LAURA (*sobbing*): Dick, Dick, you don't know what you're doing.

RICHARD (*to Weaver*): I tell you for the last time, if you'll let a sick child suffer, I won't. [*Crosses to Weaver.*] While you're out there doing your bloody work tonight what is going to happen to that man's child? Have you thought of that? What of the little girl?

WEAVER: What of your family, Dick? What of your cousin Joe who lies dead with a Gudger bullet in him? What of your Uncle Tom, what of me? It's your family, son. (*With a note of sternness.*) And one of them was killed tonight. Come, Dick [*False start.*], we must go.

RICHARD: I'll not go, I tell you. [*Breaks away.*] I'll not go. Did you send me away to prepare me for this bloody game? Haven't you seen enough murder eating through this family? Didn't my mother die because— [*Laura to chair L.*]

WEAVER (*hoarsely*): Stop, Dick!

RICHARD (*controlling himself*): I'm sorry, pa. I didn't mean to say that. But I can't go out there with you. I can't and I won't. Every principle, every fine thing I hold in my heart depends on what I do now. And I won't surrender them to carry on a fight that means nothing but murder for its own sake, murder because of the quarrel of two hot-tempered old men I never knew. I won't go! [*Richard to window, back to audience.*]

WEAVER (*with infinite sadness and tenderness*): Son [*Pause, puts hand on Richard's shoulder.*], we're like that mountaineer who thought he was a bird. [*Turns Richard slowly.*] Our fine schemes are hitched on eagle's wings.

RICHARD [*one step toward Weaver*]: We're not like Uncle Tom and his people. We got away from them.

WEAVER: It's the same stock. They're your people. We went away but we came back to them. (*Sternly.*) And one of them was killed tonight. [*False start.*] Come, Dick, we must be going.

RICHARD (*wildly*) [*draws away*]: You knew this would happen! [*Richard S. steps C.*] Why did you send me away?

WEAVER: I have no regrets. You have a place to fill here when I am gone. When I am gone, Dick, when your Uncle Tom is gone—why, then—(*He pauses.*) [*Richard back a few steps.*]

RICHARD: Then what?

WEAVER (*in a deep strong voice*): Then— Freedom! Victory! It will be your release. But not 'til then. "The old order changeth," they say. The old order never changes. It dies. (*A pause.*) I can't make you come with me. [*Goes to door.*] I shan't try. But I'm going out now to get the buggy. I'll be out front in five minutes. You can meet me there.

He goes out taking [one of the rifles from fireplace, and] his hat from Laura who stands silently in the door. Mag during all the foregoing conversation has stood awkwardly over near the fireplace. Several times she seemed about to speak but thought better of it. Now she twists her rough, toil-worn hands before her and glances quickly, furtively from Laura to Dick. Laura moves up to Richard who has turned toward the window and rests her hand lightly on his sleeve.

LAURA [*crosses to Richard*]: I'm sorry, Dick.

RICHARD (*wheeling quickly*): What's that? [*Turns a little.*] Oh!

LAURA: I'm sorry it happened so soon.

RICHARD: It doesn't matter when, I suppose.

LAURA: You mustn't blame pa, I suppose.

RICHARD: Blame him? (*Pause.*) No. I've learned to know him and to understand. (*With an ironic laugh.*)[29] How deep we think we are! How wise and original! And then we find that all our depth is not even knee-high to the other man's. [*Two steps right.*][30] O God! If I could have dreamed forever. If only—[*Crosses to Laura C.*] (*Turning desperately to her.*) Laura, Laura, I'm beginning to give in to it.[31] Is there no getting away from it?

LAURA: Not from your family, Dick.

RICHARD [*Richard turns to window*]: It's not the family. It's those accursed mountains.

LAURA [*takes Dick by arms, turns him*]: Pa,—Dick! Think of him. He's an old man. You can't let him go out there alone.

RICHARD [*pause—low tone*] (*after a desperate moment*): No! [*turns, drops hands.*] I can't. (*He strides resolutely to the closet and takes out the rifle, filling his pockets carelessly with cartridges, speaking absently all the while.*) I suppose it's in good shape. (*He snaps the barrel down and squints through it. In a quiet voice.*) O God, they are drawing me in!

LAURA [*confirmation in her voice*]: Dick, you are going with them?

RICHARD: I was a prophet in the wilderness too soon. The mountains aren't ready to receive the prophets. [*Laura C. back.*]

LAURA (*dry-eyed but choking*): It's too bad, Dick.

RICHARD (*jeering himself cruelly*): The mountains wouldn't come to Mahomet Weaver. Mahomet Weaver must go to the mountains. And the mountains are laughing tonight, Laura. They've just played one of their little jokes. And they think it's very funny. (*He goes to the window and calls out loudly.*) You think it's very funny, don't you?

LAURA (*in terror*): Dick, Dick! [*To Dick at window.*]

RICHARD [*in the same loud voice*]: Bald Pate! Bald Pate! By God, he's grinning at me! (*Mockingly.*) It's all right, Bald Pate. Go ahead and laugh. It's now the proper time to laugh.

---

29. Deletion of "I was bringing the lamp of wisdom home."
30. Deletion of "He has covered me like a tent with his own knowledge."
31. Deletion of "Great God."

(*His father's voice outside:* "*I'm waiting on you, Dick.*")

MAG (*speaking for the first time*): Hit's too bad, Dick, but I reckon ye'd better go. I ain't never seen no way out of hit.

LAURA: Go quick. They're waiting on you.

RICHARD: That's where they get you. They can wait the longest. (*He goes quickly to the door.*)

LAURA: You are going with them.

RICHARD (*with a rasping laugh*): There's nothing else to do. I've learned early. You always go with them when they want you. (*He goes out.*)

LAURA: When they want you? (*With sudden understanding turns* [*to window*].) The Mountains—(*sobbing.*) Mag, Mag, why is it? Why has it got to be?

MAG [*at fireplace*] (*dully*): Land, child, don't ask me why hit is. I don't know. (*In hard, cracked, sullen tones.*) I don't know nothin'. I reckon Tom don't think me fit fer nothin' except to do the chores an' raise a family. Now I'm an ole worn-out woman an' he'll go out thar an' like as not git killed. But does he think of me? Land, child, don't ask me why things is like they air. I reckon thar ain't no way o' findin' out.

CURTAIN

THE MOUNTAINS

A DRAMA IN THREE
ACTS AND A PROLOGUE

by Thomas Wolfe

[CHARACTERS (*in order of appearance*)

    GRAN'PAW WEAVER
    TOM WEAVER (*as a boy*)   ⎱
    BEN WEAVER   ⎰   (*Prologue*)
    GUDGER
    TWO MEN
    LAURA WEAVER, *a doctor's wife*
    BESSIE SMATHERS, *a mountaineer's wife*
    MAG, *a mountain girl*
    DR. DAVIS, *Laura's father*
    RICHARD WEAVER, *a young doctor*
    TOM WEAVER, *a mountain farmer*
    SAM, *his younger son*
    REESE, *his older son*
    LAURA   ⎱ *Richard and Laura Weaver's*
    RICHARD ⎰ *daughter and son*
    WILL GUDGER
    ROBERTS
    DAVE]

PROLOGUE

SCENE: *On a hillside.*

On an afternoon early in Spring two men and a boy are building a fence in a field which would look from a distance like a raw brown patch climbing the steep flanks of a hill. The ragged edges of the field are embraced by the encircling pine woods which cover the rest of the hill. The soil is poor and stony, and of a clayey color like the weather-baked skins of the fence builders.

It is at the end of March and, though the Spring comes early here, a strong wind blows through the pines, and snakes in vast curves through the long grass in the field.

Receding into the mists at the horizon's edge are interlapping ranges of blue mountains, to the nearest of which this hill provides the approach. Crows wheel cawing around the field; from the distance at the left comes intermittently the faint sound of cowbells in the valley. There is thin smoke over the tops of the pines at the right indicating a dwelling nearby.

The older of the two men is well over sixty. He is lean almost to gauntness and great corded veins rise out of his sinewy hands. His form is tall but stooped and he never looks around or pauses from the work he is doing. The younger man is of middle age; he, too, is gaunt and bent, and works with stolid indifference to everything but the fence. They do not talk to each other as they work, but silently lift the logs or nail the crossed uprights through which the log bars run.

The boy, not over fourteen years of age, stands by restlessly, helping little in the work but showing himself a lively fellow by the interest he takes in everything that is going on. He looks up at the crows with interest, listens attentively when he hears the cow-bells, and occasionally, acting on a sudden impulse, picks up a stone and hurls it down the hill with all his strength, listening to its bounding course with keen attention.

THE OLD MAN (*straightening up, with his hands pressed to his back*): Fetch the jug, sonny. I want some water.

(*The boy runs off to the left and returns presently with a brown earthen jug. The Old Man drinks and gives the jug to the younger man, who drinks.*)

THE BOY (*curiously*): Whar do the jugs come from, Gran'-paw?

GRAN'PAW: Jugtown, sonny.

THE BOY (*with close interest*): Whar's that?

GRAN'PAW (*with an indefinite gesture*): Oh, out yonder.

(*Faint and far in the distance a train whistle blows.*)

Now, help tote this log, Tommy. Night-time's gittin' on.

(*The three lift a heavy log and lay it between the forks in silence.*)

TOMMY (*suddenly*): I reckon thar's a power o' jugs in Jugtown, ain't thar?

GRAN'PAW (*surprised*): Wal!

(*He winks good-naturedly at the other man.*)

More'n ye could tote away with a two-hoss wagon, Tommy.

(*Squinting at the sun.*)

Hit's atter four. We'll be gittin' on. We orter be up to the edge o' the clearing by night.

(*The boy, meanwhile, fidgets around, and wanders off. The younger man recalls him peremptorily.*)

THE YOUNGER MAN: You, Tom, come back hyeh, an' lend a hand.

GRAN'PAW (*quietly*): Leave the boy be, Ben. We don't need his help. He's gittin' spring-time in his bones an' wants to kick up his heels. He'll grow up to man's work soon enough.

(*With strong teeth he tears off a huge chunk of tobacco from a twisted plug. The train-whistle sounds again in the distance, now very faint. The boy listens.*)

TOMMY: Gran'paw, did ye ever see the cyars?

GRAN'PAW: Onct.

TOMMY: Ye never rode on 'em, did ye?

GRAN'PAW: No, I hain't an' I don't never intend to. Hit ain't safe.

TOMMY: Whar do the cyars go, Gran'paw?

GRAN'PAW (*with the same indefinite gesture*): Out thar.

BEN (*sharply*): Don't ask yore granpap so many fool questions!

GRAN'PAW (*in a quiet aside, as before*): Don't plague him, Ben. He's at the p'int when he hankers to know things. The sap's risin' in him, I reckon.

TOMMY (*who has brooded deeply over each bit of information given him*): I reckon as how the cyars go to Jugtown, don't they?

GRAN'PAW: I reckon as how they do. (*Goes on working.*)

TOMMY: I'd like to ride on the cyars.

(*There is no reply to this. The men continue to work. Presently the boy wanders off again.*)

BEN (*to the old man*): How d'ye reckon ole man Gudger'll take yore fencin' the land?

GRAN'PAW: Dunno. What's he got to do with hit? Hit's my land, hain't it?

BEN: Yeah. Only thar ain't never been no fence—

GRAN'PAW: Wal, thar's goin' to be one from now on. I want to git hit settled what's my own an' what's his'n.

BEN: I heerd tell at the sto' as how he said hit was his'n.

GRAN'PAW: 'S a damn lie. My paw gave me this land.

BEN (*quietly*): I wouldn't have words with ole man Gudger ef I was you, paw. You been neighbors a long time an' a few foot of land one way or 'other hain't wuth argyin' ovah.

GRAN'PAW (*snorting angrily*): Well, I hain't goin' to be done out of what's mine ef hit hain't wuth a penny.

BEN: Hit's mighty pore land, anyway. Hit won't raise beans. Mountain land!

(*They work on silently for a short time and the neighbor, Gudger, a florid-faced old man with long moustaches, appears on the other side of the fence. He watches the work for a moment without speaking. They nod to him and go on. Finally:—*)

GUDGER: Reckon thar's a mistake, ain't thar, neighbor?

GRAN'PAW (*shortly*): No. I reckon not.

GUDGER: It 'pears to me ye're a leetle ovah on my side.

GRAN'PAW (*pausing and looking up*): Mebbe the hull field's yourn.

GUDGER (*unruffled*): No. I don't say that. I say ye've made a mistake an' come ovah a leetle on my side. Yore line runs from yon pine to the side o' the rock up thar.

GRAN'PAW: I reckon I know whar my line runs. The pine ain't got nothin' to do with hit. I'm layin' my fence from the spring down thar which is accordin to what my paw told me.

GUDGER: Ef yore paw said that, Weaver, he was wrong. The spring's on my land an' allus has been. I don't grudge yore usin' the spring. Use hit an' welcome, same's you allus done. But ye're fencin' in my land now an' that ain't right. I'm a man as believes in doin' the right thing. Right's right an' wrong's wrong! (*Rather heatedly.*) The land mebbe ain't good fer nothin' much but hit's mine an' ye've no business fencin' hit.

BEN (*interposing quietly*): Hit hain't wuth argyin' ovah, Mister Gudger. Mebbe you er paw's got papers that'll show which is right, one way or t'other.

GUDGER (*rather violently*): No. I hain't got no papers an' I don't need none. I know what's mine.

GRAN'PAW (*ironically*): Hit looks like hit! Mebbe your brother Jim knew what was his'n when he was jailed fer takin' a [ham].

BEN (*sharply*): Paw! Don't go on like that now.

(*Gudger reddens with anger.*)

Hit's all right, Mister Gudger.

GUDGER: All right! Since ye said that, I ain't goin' to fool no more with ye. Git back on yore own side an' take this fence down, or I'll tear hit down. I don't want no more doin's with the likes of you. Now, git off my land.

OLD WEAVER: Who said hit was yourn?

GUDGER: I say so, by God!

OLD WEAVER: Ye don't need to git sassy now. Ye ain't got no call to go gittin' on yore head 'bout hit.

GUDGER: Air ye goin' to git off like I told ye?

OLD WEAVER: No, an' what's more this hyeh fence is goin' to stay jest like I built hit an' I'd better not catch ye meddlin' with hit.

GUDGER (*slowly*): We'll see about that. When I come back, ef I find ye hyeh I'll run ye off.

(*He goes off rapidly.*)

OLD WEAVER (*jeering after him*): I'd like to see ye try hit.

BEN (*exasperated*): Now, ye've done hit. What'd you go an' talk 'bout his brother [Jim] like that fer? Ye might've knowed hit would rile him.

OLD WEAVER: Well, hit's true, hain't it? Everybody knows his brother stole a smoked ham out'n ole man Rutherford's smoke house an' got jailed fer hit.

BEN: Well, that ain't his fault. His brother never was no 'count. An' what's hit got to do with the land, anyway? He's yore neighbor, an' we've got to live by him. I call hit a bad day's work.

OLD WEAVER: Things happen sudden like that. An' ef they've got to be, they've got to be, an' we cain't change 'em. I done what I thought was right. No man's more tolable then I be. But he ain't goin' to tear my fence down.

BEN: Old Gudger's mule-headed. An' you ain't easy to argy with. He'll hold this agin' ye a long time.

OLD WEAVER: That may be. But I'll attend to what's mine, no matter what happens. I don't aim to be walked on.

(*Gudger appears armed with a rifle.*)

BEN: Paw, let's go. The ole man's riled. We'll settle this peaceable when ye've both toned down.

GUDGER: I told ye to git off, didn't I? Am I goin' to have to drive ye off at the p'int of a gun?

OLD WEAVER: Ye don't scare me none with yore squirrel gun. Gudger, ye'd better leave me be. I've had enough of yore goin's-on now. I ain't goin' to fergit the way ye acted this day.

GUDGER: Git off, you land thief.

OLD WEAVER (*stung to fury*): Damn you. Don't call me no name like that.

(*He starts forward.*)

BEN: Paw! (*Restrains him. To Gudger.*) Ye don't know what ye're doin', Mister Gudger. Nor him neither. Ye're ole men an' easy riled. Now, go on away an' I'll take him home. We'll fix this thing peaceable when both of ye have toned down some.

OLD WEAVER: I'll tone him down ef he opens his dirty mouth to me agin.

GUDGER: I've took enough off'n you. Air ye goin'?

OLD WEAVER: I'll see ye in hell afore I move. Thief yoreself. Yore brother was a thief an' ye're no better.

BEN: Paw. (*Tries to lead him away.*) Come on, paw, come on. Ye ain't in yore right senses.

OLD WEAVER: Yes, he is! Tryin' to take what's mine. I'll show him if he can, the—

GUDGER (*shouting, mad with anger*): Git off! Git off! Ye won't? Then—by God!

(*Shoots. Old Weaver falls, his face toward the earth. The jug is overturned and broken. Ben kneels at his father's side.*)

BEN: Air ye hurt bad, paw?

(*The old man is dead. The boy, Tom, runs in and stops short with horror. Gudger, his smoking gun across the fence bars, stands silently watching. The boy attempts to run to where his grandfather lies but is restrained by Ben, who, looking steadily at Gudger, goes slowly off. Two men of Gudger's come running up. He speaks curtly to them.*)

GUDGER: Tear this fence down.

(*Shocked at the sight of the still figure, they mechanically lift the top bar and throw it off. Old Weaver lies with his face turned to the earth. The train whistle blows far off.*)

CURTAIN

ACT I

SCENE: *The living room in the home of Weaver, a mountain doctor.*

The house is a substantial country dwelling, the most pretentious in this lonely region, equipped with most of those devices for comfort we call "conveniences." The illumination, however, is furnished by oil lamps.

The furniture is of dark walnut, somewhat ornate after those designs that found favor (and gave comfort) twenty or thirty years ago.

Since the magic of psychology now permits us to read a man's character by examining his furniture, even as the Greeks read omens by inspecting animals' entrails, Dr. Weaver's living room may be said to reflect subtly the personalities of fine but opposite people who live here. It is well-worn and comfortable, pervaded by dark and mellow tones; it bears definitely the impress of qualities of strength and sweetness.

There is a hearth and mantel at the left. The mantel bears an old wooden clock and two vases at either end. The hearth is wide and deep, capable of burning whole logs. It has massive, brightly polished brass andirons and the heavy brass-headed poker, tongs, and shovel lean against the sides from hooks driven for this purpose. There are wide double windows at the back which give a sweeping view of the landscape. At the center there is a table on which are magazines, papers, a few books, and a knitting basket. There are chairs on each side of the table.

Dr. Weaver's old walnut desk is at the back slightly to the left of the windows where there is a good light. At the right is a large, glass-covered book case with shelves stored with heavy calfskin medical books.

The floor is entirely carpeted with one rug. The single entry to the room is through a door at the back wall over to the right wall. It gives on a hall which runs through the house.

The door is open and discloses a table with a wooden hat-rack of the fold-up accordion variety, which hangs above the table.

There are two travelling bags, over which a light overcoat is thrown, at the side of the table.

It is toward sundown of a day late in September. Through the broad windows at the back a view of the mountain landscape is disclosed burnished by the red glow of the sun which is just dropping behind the horizon. The foliage has but lately begun to turn to autumn colors. By the view through the window, it is evident that Weaver's house is built on the side of a hill which drops down to a narrow valley, bounded on the other side by hills and by great wooded ranges of mountains which recede in overlapping waves into the background.

So remote is the last visible range of the mountains that it seems shrouded continually in ghostly mists through which the eye cannot pierce. In the middle distance, apparently isolated from the other mountains, is a granite peak, a curious natural malformation, whose stark outlines suggest strangely the profile of an old, hook-nosed, sardonically grinning man.

From the valley may be heard the occasional sounds of cowbells and somewhere in the distance there is the sound of a springless wagon jolting slowly over a rough road. One can also catch a glimpse of polished steel rails running along the flanks of the hill a few hundred feet below the house. The trains go by twice a day, stopping for a noisy moment at the little station just out of one's sight to the left.

The view is ordinarily undisturbed by signs of any human activity, but it could not be described as "peaceful." Rather it is mighty in its great repose and quiet depth.

Already the light begins to rush from the house. The shadows move swiftly across the little valley and up the hills until finally only the upper parts of the mountains remain bathed in the golden light. Soon darkness will be there as well.

There is a knocking outside and Mrs. Weaver, a pretty, graceful woman, twenty-eight years old, goes through the hall and opens the outer door. She returns to the living room presently with a mountain woman who bears a child, swaddled in ragged blankets. The woman is a gaunt, starved creature, not old but of indefinable age, whose sullen features are stamped with the mark not only of privation and misery but with a fierce and untamed pride, as well. The face of the child is not visible.

MRS. WEAVER: You wish to see Dr. Weaver, I suppose?

THE WOMAN: Yes'm. Is he in?

MRS. WEAVER: No, the doctor is out making visits. He will return soon, I think. Can I give him any message?

THE WOMAN: No. I reckon not. What time d'ye cal'c'late he'll get back?

MRS. WEAVER: I cannot tell you that. But I think it will be by eight o'clock surely. Won't you give me your name so that I can tell him?

THE WOMAN: Thar ain't no need. (*Briefly.*) I'm Bessie Smathers. He knows me. I reckon I'll be goin'. (*She starts to go.*) I'll come back later on.

(*There is something suggestive of such poignant misery in her dull, sullen face that Mrs. Weaver feels impelled to question her:*)

MRS. WEAVER (*gently*): You seem to be in trouble. Won't you tell me what it is?

BESSIE (*sullenly*): You cain't help me none. I want the doc. My baby's ailin' (*with increased rapidity of speech*). I don't know what's wrong with 'im. He don't make no noise. I'm might-nigh crazy. He jest looks at me.

(*Ashamed suddenly of her outburst, she lapses into sullen silence.*)

MRS. WEAVER: Won't you let me see the baby?

(*She makes a movement as if to take the child in her arms, but the woman withdraws a step or two like a startled animal, holding the child tightly. Mrs. Weaver makes no further attempt but tries to reassure her.*)

He will be here soon, don't worry. Won't you sit down and wait for him?

BESSIE: No. Hit ain't fer to whar I live. I'll go home an' come back.

MRS. WEAVER: I'll tell him as soon as he returns. (*The woman goes.*) Goodbye.

(*She follows her to the door and presently returns.*)

(*Mag, a mountain girl, enters, bearing a lamp, which she places on the table. Mag is a rather tall, raw-boned girl of eighteen years, with homely features, tightly knotted hair, and hands already roughened and enlarged by hard toil. She is dressed in a shapeless, ill-hanging gingham dress.*)

(*She gets a match from a box on the mantel and lights the lamp. It gives only a half light to the room.*)

MRS. WEAVER: Can't we have more light, Mag?

MAG: Hain't this all right?

MRS. WEAVER: I like a cheerful light. These wretched lamps! Everything looks so gloomy. (*Shivering a little.*) Will you run upstairs and fetch my shawl?

MAG (*in wonder*): Lord! Mrs. Weaver. Ye ain't cold this airly in the year? Mebbe ye'll like a fire?

MRS. WEAVER: Oh, no. It's not cold enough for that. I'm just a little chilled. The shawl will do. (*Mag starts to go. Mrs. Weaver interrupts her casually.*) And, oh, Mag! Couldn't you arrange to

get here a little earlier in the morning? It was nearly nine o'clock
before you came to-day.

(*Dr. Davis, her father, enters.*)

MAG (*frankly*): No, ma'am, I cain't, less'n you take to gittin' up airlier. Maw says not to do a lick o' work long's ye air layin'
in bed.

MRS. WEAVER (*quietly*): Very well, Mag. We'll try to manage it.

(*Mag goes out. Mrs. Weaver turns smilingly to her father.
Davis, a man of fifty-five, is a prosperous, efficient city physician
with a well-to-do clientele. He is a florid clean-shaven man, of
medium height, swift and dynamic in his movements, assured in
his bearing, and with a professional geniality which does not con-
ceal the fact that he has only so much time for everyone. His eyes
are hard, brilliant and piercing—these are likewise the qualities most
characteristic of his mind. Beneath his reserve and impassivity, he
is capable of deeper emotion than one would suspect. Not ir-
religious, but substituting for religion that which he understands
in the light of known evidence—something he calls "the Process."
Not cynical, but a sceptic, by reason of a complete devotion to
the one thing he respects, the Fact. He is a hard man to talk faith
to, or belief in the supernatural objects, for he has constructed his
whole opinion of life from evidence he has seen and tested. If to
this account it is added that he reads Greek in moments of relaxa-
tion, quotes Plato out of respect to his calibre and not from agreement, and thinks parts of the Bible are great literature, one may
accomplish a fair understanding of a man broadly, not narrowly,
scientific.*)

DAVIS (*referring to the just departed Mag*): You might be
working for her, instead of her working for you. Why do you put
up with it? Give her her wages and let her go.

MRS. WEAVER: What's the use? It's their pride. They all
have it. If I get anyone in her place, it'll probably be the same.

DAVIS: A queer bunch. A strange life they lead here. Eh,
Lord!

MRS. WEAVER: Oh, when you get used to their ways, they're not bad. Mag works hard and faithfully as long as I keep busy. But if I start to loaf, you've got to watch her.

DAVIS: But, damn it, Laura, you're not trying out a new experiment in government. The woman's your servant; you pay her; and she's here to do what you tell her to do without asking questions.

(*Mag returns with the shawl which Mrs. Weaver places around her shoulders.*)

MRS. WEAVER: I have no idea when Dr. Weaver will return, Mag. He drove over to Beaverdam to-day. It's getting dark now. You may go home if you want to.

MAG: Thankee. I'll wait a spell. Tom's comin' to take me home. (*She goes out.*)

DAVIS: Who's Tom?

MRS. WEAVER (*after a moment—with a faint smile*): He's my—brother-in-law.

DAVIS: Is he—on friendly terms—with this girl?

MRS. WEAVER: Decidedly! He's "setting up" to her, as they say.

DAVIS: Ha! Well, this *is* democracy!

MRS. WEAVER: Let me show you something, father.

(*She goes to the table and takes a folded piece of paper from a book.*)

My brother-in-law also composed poetry. I found this in here the other day. He wrote it for Mag.

(*She gives Davis the paper. He reads in bewilderment, and chuckles.*)

DAVIS: But, good heavens, this is ridiculous! (*Reads aloud.*) "I love you once, I love you twice, I love you as much as Jesus Christ."

MRS. WEAVER: I laughed, too, when I read it. But I didn't let Mag see me. There's something deadly earnest about these people, especially when a man sets out to find his woman. There's not much foolishness about them.

DAVIS: Your position is a unique one, Laura. Your friends would be surprised if they knew.

MRS. WEAVER: Yes, I suppose they would be. But so would I have been five years ago.

DAVIS: These mountains are beautiful—but God-forsaken, my dear. (*A pause.*) Are you quite happy here?

(*A longer pause; then faint and far in the distance a train-whistle blows.*)

MRS. WEAVER: There comes your train, father.

DAVIS: Good Lord. Then I must hurry. However, my cases are packed.

MRS. WEAVER: You have lots of time, father. He's at the foot of the mountain. It will be a half hour before they climb the grade. And the station isn't three minutes from here. Father, must you go tonight?

DAVIS: Yes, dear. I'm afraid I must. You see, I'm a very busy man since I got my hospital. Two weeks is as much as I can spare.

MRS. WEAVER: It was good of you to come. You just seemed to bring the old life with you. (*Suddenly she puts her arms around him and kisses him.*) Oh, but I shall miss you now.

DAVIS (*quietly*): Sit down, Laura.

(*He sits beside her on the lounge and draws her over on his shoulder, the while he speaks gently and coaxingly to her.*)

You get lonesome, eh? Yes, I thought so. And Dick is away on his visits a good part of the time, isn't he?

MRS. WEAVER: He has to work so hard, the poor boy.

DAVIS: Yes, he has enough work for two men. He's bitten off more than he can chew. Now, then. There is no one whom you can talk to, no theatres, libraries, shops, or social life, wherewith you can amuse yourself. These people are not your kind; and you are certainly not theirs. After five years you know them no better. Isn't this right?

(*After a moment she nods slowly.*)

Laura, it is sheer folly for Dick to keep on here. That fellow is a great surgeon. They told me at Johns Hopkins he was the most promising specimen they'd had in years. With the pair of hands he's got, he'd make a fortune. I want you to come back. There's work enough in my hospital alone for Dick and myself, and I'll take him in whatever time he decides to come. Will you talk to him?

MRS. WEAVER: It would be no use, father. You know how Dick feels about staying here. These people are terribly ignorant; they get sick and die in droves unless someone's here to look after them. He told me once he'd feel like a deserter if he left them. Dick's thoroughly fine and I love him for it.

DAVIS: That's quite true. I'm sure we all appreciate that. But idealism must be mixed with common sense if it's to get anywhere. You needn't look at me as if I were propounding an arch-heresy. It's quite possible to be comfortable and do good work, too. I believe Dick could be of more service in a big city hospital than here.

MRS. WEAVER: Why do you think that?

DAVIS: In the first place it's a wise idea for a young fellow to strike out for himself in a new place. I never thought of going back to my home when I got through the Medical School. Get away from your family. Let them admire you from a distance; the greater the distance, the more will they admire you. I have noticed one thing up here. The family tie seems to be extraordinarily strong. A man is apt to lose his individuality in that kind of a connection, if he doesn't mind. Besides, I've heard talk since I came of some kind of trouble between Dick's people and some other mountain family.

MRS. WEAVER: The Gudgers. But that's an old quarrel. Dick laughs at it. There has been no trouble for years. Besides, Dick would have no part in it if there were. You can't expect him to feel the same as some ignorant, backwoods mountaineer.

DAVIS: Perhaps not. Still, all that counts against his success here. Especially if the other tribe, or faction, or what-not, look on him as a member of his clan. He has a hard and thankless job ahead of him unless he does the sensible thing and comes with me. Won't you try to talk him into it?

MRS. WEAVER: Oh, but I hate to say anything to him. He's

been so strong and brave. Yet I know he's worried and worked half to death. If I should nag at him, it would only add to his troubles.

DAVIS: Laura, you have two children to think of. In a few years they'll be old enough for school. Do you want to keep them shut in from the world and from an education?

MRS. WEAVER: No, I don't. That's what makes it so hard now when I think of it. I could stand it better if there were just the two of us. But I want little Dick and Laura to have all the things I had. Life here is so terribly primitive, so lonely.

DAVIS: Then you must tell that to Dick.

MRS. WEAVER. I'm worried about him, too. I think the pace he goes is telling on him. He gets so discouraged. And—he's becoming just a little hard, I'm afraid. When we came here, I marvelled at his patience. Things were always happening to try him, but he was so sweet and gentle and patient with everyone that there seemed to be no end to his good-humor. (*She sighs.*) He was such a fine big boy then. And in five years!

DAVIS: Yes, he has changed. That's what happens to us when we get iron in our soul.

MRS. WEAVER: Oh, but he's more determined than ever. But he looks so grim at times. These people are so ignorant. He will leave medicine and they won't take it. They'll listen to his instructions and then won't follow them. A few weeks ago something happened, just a little thing, that almost broke his endurance for the time, I think. He stayed up and walked the floor half the night.

DAVIS: What was it?

MRS. WEAVER: He left medicine for a woman who had a cold and a very severe cough. When he went out again, he found her husband hadn't given his medicine at all but was dosing her on some quack cure—all pills he'd bought of a medicine man at the fair.

DAVIS: He can fight disease, but he'll find it a harder matter to fight superstition. And when it's bred in the bone! It's a tough proposition, I'm afraid.

MRS. WEAVER: That was almost the last straw at the time. He couldn't sleep, he couldn't eat for several days. And since then he's seemed more grim than ever. I've heard him give several of his patients dreadful calling-downs. He never used to be like that.

DAVIS (*consulting his watch*): I do hope he returns in time to see me off.

MRS. WEAVER: Something has delayed him, I know. (*Carriage wheels outside.*) I believe he's here now. He'll see you off, after all.

(*Weaver enters. At this time Dr. Weaver is a man of thirty-two years, already inclining toward corpulency, florid, decisive in his movements, his strong features are already scarred, his deep, searching eyes already a little tired from the uneven contest that is being waged between what is within and what is without him. His voice has a hearty ring.*)

WEAVER: God forgive me, father Davis, but I thought I'd miss you after all. I drove the mare into a white sweat on the way home. (*Embraces his wife.*) How are you, dear? You look mighty solemn. Father, be a good boy and wait over till morning. It's so much more cheerful sending you away in the daylight. And the view from the train of our highly advertised mountain scenery is rather good, if you like that sort of thing.

DAVIS: Sorry, Dick. But I've procrastinated enough. I *must* go to-night.

MRS. WEAVER: What kept you so long, dear?

WEAVER (*looking weary suddenly*): Oh, the usual thing. I went out to see one patient and found a half-dozen more. There's a woman out on Beaverdam down with incipient pneumonia, her three children are whooping and sniffling and coughing, her brute of a husband is off on a jag, and everything in that house is one damn mess. I got one of her neighbors to come over and tend to her, and left her after stuffing her head with instructions I don't expect her to keep. Hey-ho! It's a great life we lead here, isn't it?

DAVIS: There's a good deal of pneumonia out in the mountains, isn't there, Dick?

WEAVER (*a look of pain crossing his face*): I tell you it's awful. You have no idea of what's going on out there. The poor devils sicken and die like beasts, and like beasts they make no sound. When Death comes, they turn their faces to the wall and let go.

(*He passes his hand involuntarily before his eyes as if to blot out some awful vision.*)

DAVIS (*kindly*): You need a rest, Dick.

WEAVER (*waving his hand impatiently*): Not now! Not now! This is the sick time of the year. Those rains did the trick. Good Lord, I wonder if there are any well people left in the world.

(*Mrs. Weaver starts to go out.*)

Where are you going, dear?

MRS. WEAVER: I'll give you and father the chance to talk a while. Shall we have supper now or later? Father's had his supper.

WEAVER (*looking at his watch*): Then, if you don't mind, we'll wait until he has gone.

DAVIS: What martyrdom! (*Looking at his watch.*) However, it's only a matter of twenty minutes, Dick, and I want to talk to you.

(*Mrs. Weaver goes out.*)

WEAVER: Good. I'm sorry we're so pressed for time. It was unavoidable.

(*They seat themselves comfortably and are silent for a moment. Mrs. Weaver returns to the door.*)

MRS. WEAVER: Richard—a woman came here asking for you.

WEAVER: Did she leave her name?

MRS. WEAVER: Her name is Bessie Smathers. She had a sick baby. She said she'd return later.

WEAVER: Thank you, dear. (*She goes out.*) There's a case for you! This woman has been too sick to work and she's too proud to accept help from her neighbors. As a result of her stubbornness, the child isn't getting enough to eat. I've tried to talk to her, but it's no use. What am I to do?

DAVIS: Where's her husband?

WEAVER: God knows. He's selling cheap whiskey all around.

But she hasn't seen him for months. He knows her condition but evidently doesn't care what becomes of her. I happen to know he hasn't given a penny to her support for months. Damned brute!

DAVIS: Exactly. A damned brute. But it's an impossible situation. You've done your duty. Why worry about it?

WEAVER: If you could see the child! He's a tenacious little fellow. Courage, you never saw the like of it. You can count his ribs, but I've never heard a yip from him. It's awful to see suffering like that.

DAVIS (*very seriously*): Suffering like that, my dear boy, is inevitable.

WEAVER: No, no. You can't make me believe that. Stupidity and ignorance is at the bottom of such suffering.

DAVIS: As Socrates would say: What does that prove? Stupidity and ignorance are inevitable. When you attempt to explain one thing in terms of something else you are no nearer the truth than before.

WEAVER (*derisively*): This is a fine way for a man of science to talk! Such things ought not to be. There ought to be a way of stopping them.

DAVIS: Ought! Ought! What have we to do with that? When I was in college, eighty or ninety years ago, we had an old chemistry professor who was commonly called a "fogey." The old fellow was forever making his experiments before us and they never came out right. The flame wasn't good or the solution would solute—something was always the matter. Finally he'd give it up and say, "Well, anyway, it ought to come out right."

WEAVER: And, as Socrates would say: What does that prove?

DAVIS: It proves that there are elements quite beyond your power of regulation. You dream of that far distant time when science will have stamped out, one by one, the causes of these plagues and miseries that wreck the world. You even dream of its ultimate triumph over ignorance and superstition, and finally, perhaps, over death—death, that is, from disease or decay. But consider for one moment: one thing that makes life tolerable is the fact we may lose it in so many different ways. (*With irony.*)

Reduce the ways in which a man could lose his life to one—let us say—pneumonia—and he'd spend his days in fear and his nights in woolen pajamas.

WEAVER: That is a queer argument. You seem to deny progress.

DAVIS: No, no. Let's have it, by all means. Anything to make life more tolerable. But you can't do away with the facts that plague us. Others are forever springing up in their place.

WEAVER: Do you still worship your little gods—the Facts?

DAVIS: Why not? I believe you worship something so mysterious, I've never been able to understand it—something you call your faith.

WEAVER: Yes, I do.

DAVIS: If you'll excuse me, I'll keep my facts and you may have your faith. I'm well satisfied with the division. And yet, do you know, Dick, you've changed considerably in five years. I sometimes wonder if you haven't lost your faith.

WEAVER: No. People change, I suppose. Perhaps we grow. Yet we have longings to return. I sometimes look for the boy in the man. And I can't find him although he's there. Ten includes five, said the philosopher: it has all that five has except the capacity to be five. You have noticed that I seem hard, a little bitter, maybe. (*Davis nods.*) It's not that I've lost my faith. It's simply that I've had to fight for it. And what we fight for, we cherish.

DAVIS: Things keep going wrong, don't they?

WEAVER: Yes. But that's our fault. I never see misery, disease, or wretched people but what I am convinced the causes of their distress may be eradicated by human effort. It does no good to blame these things on Fate and Destiny. I don't understand such talk. I have always believed in law; in law that is supreme and universal and, more than that, kindly. That is my faith.

DAVIS: My dear boy. I've been a physician too long to be taken in with any high-sounding talk about a kind and equable operation in our universe. You can't speculate about the unknowable unless you're prepared to face the facts. You have no right to hold your ghostly house on any foundations save those you see around you.

WEAVER: What do you mean?

DAVIS: I mean if you try to know what is unknown you have to draw your conclusions from the evidence you see. If the visible universe is bad, and filled with ugly and cancerous objects, a cold and merciless logic compels you to unpleasant conclusions about the invisible universe. You have eyes to see. You know what you know. Yet you build a fairy castle founded on something you call your faith, which has no basis either in reason or observation. Out of this mysterious and unreal faith you draw a glorious scheme of things which you ask me to accept as reality but by what inter-mediation you bring about this miracle you can not form even an intelligent conjecture.

WEAVER: Such an argument might convince me if I were willing to admit that what we see is ugly and loathsome as you say. But I will not admit that I do not think it is true.

DAVIS (*impatiently*): Is the testimony of your senses a lie? Do your eyes lie to you? No, you're a physician and in a position to get the truth. Illusions have no place in a doctor's life. Be honest with yourself. When you look around you, what do you see every-where? Happiness? Contentment? Prosperity? No. The one thing you see and know, the one thing that touches us all, that none es-capes, that is everywhere around us is—Suffering! That is the uni-versal experience.

WEAVER: No, no! I won't believe that. I tell you life is beau-tiful and kindly. If we suffer, it is only that we may love it more.

DAVIS: That is interesting. Do you appreciate your teeth more for having the tooth-ache?

WEAVER: Oh, you're a good debater, doctor, but you can't break my faith.

DAVIS (*dryly*): No, I suppose not. It's about all you have left to argue with.

WEAVER: You would deny the presence of unity and order. You would look on the world as a mad shambles of suffering and destruction. But it can't be true.

DAVIS: But it is. A child skipping down the road can, by a whim, change its pace or direction so as to give life or death to ten thousand things that creep and crawl and build their homes on the earth as you do. Do you see unity, order, or a plan there? You cannot take a walk over the nearest hillside to view the beauty of this beneficent nature you talk of without leaving murder in your footsteps. Death may come to you from a thousand unexpected sources. It may drop its poison in the spring from which you drink; it may spread a plague through the air you breathe. Yet there are people who profess to see a divine order in this, who believe that not a sparrow falls to the ground in vain, that Providence (whatever that may be) is at your elbow guiding every act. What abominable cant! Why are men forever denying the truth? Life is too strong for us. We haven't the courage to face it. And it overpowers us. We refuse the testimony of the things we see and know. We profess to believe in the impossible when the evidence is before our eyes.

WEAVER: You talk this way because you're a physician. You have seen so much of the world's pain that you take a one-sided view of things.

DAVIS: I recognize the danger. But this is everywhere. We don't have to be doctors to see it. Let's have no nonsense about optimism. If you're going to be that kind of Fool, go read the verses in the newspaper, such as "a cheerful smile makes life worth while," or "if you think you can do it, you can" or "just buckle right in with a bit of a grin." That is what they call "optimism," I believe.

WEAVER: You would make suffering the end, the goal of life?

DAVIS: Make it what you like. But admit its presence. You can't ascribe that to accident. Accidents don't happen on a universal scale.

WEAVER: But my faith—what is that? Is that an accident? I'll admit that my faith can be answered by neither of your almighty tests: reason and observation. Yet the presence of my faith is as widespread as the presence of this suffering, you speak of. All men have it.

DAVIS: Have they? Then, what does that prove?

WEAVER: It proves more than even reason or observation could prove. For we have this faith, most men, without knowing why, and its presence is a proof that accident can not answer.

DAVIS: Yes. An answer to what most men would like to believe. But don't go it blind. Use your knowledge. I'm a pessimist. I admit it. But my pessimism is sane. In fact, I think I have a better time out of life than you do, for all your faith.

WEAVER: Perhaps. But in view of what you have said, I can hardly believe it.

DAVIS: You may call this belief in suffering my creed, if you will. But it has driven me to sane conclusions. Once a man knows the presence of misery he will look about for relief.

WEAVER: For happiness.

DAVIS: No, for relief. That's all there is. Relief may be obtained by developing a taste for fine and beautiful things—for good books, good music, good pictures, good tobacco, good food.

WEAVER: A hash! A beastly, common stew!

DAVIS: If I were not a man with a profession, I think I would devote my life to the appreciation of beauty. I would read only the books that fostered it, hear only the music that conveyed it, see only the pictures that painted it.

WEAVER: And taste only the dinners that cooked it.

DAVIS: You have the idea.

WEAVER: If you were not my father-in-law, I should say your belief was that of a very fat-headed person.

DAVIS: I am grateful for your self-control.

WEAVER: But you believe no such thing. Otherwise you would retire from your profession now—you have enough money —and gratify these desires. But you keep on, and I know you are not wholly mercenary. You gouge the rich man who comes to your hospital, but there's many poor man who never pays a penny.

DAVIS: Well, we can't always get it, you know.

WEAVER: And you claim to find relief in this way. Really, I don't believe you. The most frantic people I know are the beauty-hunters. They race through life like mad donkeys chasing a bundle of hay that hangs before their nose. They narrow their vision of things so they have eyesight only for what they want to see. I knew one in the city who would walk home through the section of beautiful homes and take a cab through the slums.

DAVIS: He was loyal to his belief, then. He had the courage of his convictions.

WEAVER: He was a fool, as much so as some religious zealot who stunts his feelings in order to imagine there is no pain. There is something half-bestial, centaur-like, about this beauty cult. It is a curious mixture that hashes up the things which appeal to the mind and the senses—good books and good dinners, as you say. And always you people are frantic, restless, disturbed. You live for the fleeting moment. You try to catch it and hold it, and if you think you succeed, you go your way leaping and dancing, crying, "I have lived!" What you really mean is, "I have made my point!" for you're all propagandists. "Carpe diem," live for the present, you say. But there is no present. Even while you speak it is gone. We live in the past and the future.

DAVIS: Laugh at it all you please. There is unity in such a creed. And there is comfort there. One may be clear and sure in the point of view.

WEAVER: Yes, when we trim life according to our pattern. But it refuses to be trimmed. Perhaps you see life clearly, but you do not see it whole, in all its variety and bewildering complexity. You have accused me of overlooking the facts. Now it is my turn to accuse you of doing that. I see the facts and demand an explanation. You see them and accept them. You would retire and use only the things that appeal to the sense of beauty. I would survey the whole thing, for it appeals to something much finer and nobler —the intellect. It is fairly easy to find harmony and perfection when we see to it that our experiences come from harmonious and perfect things. But your house is made of straw; it comes down at one blow. To find unity in the heart of struggle, unity in the midst of everlasting change, unity and meaning in suffering and woe—there is the problem that can set the mind on fire, that can infuse it with a passion that will make your pretty little carnalities shine like guttering candles by comparison.

DAVIS: I see you are still refreshingly young—and ignorant. I have seen this intellect with which you would unriddle the universe. Yes, I have seen it and held it in these two hands. It is quite an ordinary looking thing with a great many curves or convolutions. I have one of them preserved in a jar of alcohol. It is so long and so wide; a finite thing with a beginning, a middle, and an end. You would make it your hero.

WEAVER: Yes. A hero—a god! Nothing is beyond its power. When my courage fails, I see it rising like a bright sword that turns in all directions over all the mass of passions, emotions and blind gropings of instincts which destroy us. It is able to search out and understand anything—even the human spirit—and it will, some day. It will.

DAVIS: I am not blind as you may think to what you have called the variety and complexity of life. I observe it, but I do not attempt to understand it. That is beyond us; there is no meaning in chaos. Men have tried, for centuries, to solve the problem you have stated. Can you name one who has answered it? Can you name one whose intellect has carried him to the answer? Is there one of them who has gone beyond the point of seeing the thing? So much, then, for the intellect. It has its uses, but it is not to find an answer to what has no answer. You see that life is complex and varied. Very well. What does that prove? It proves that life is complex and varied. That's all there is to it. There is no problem. There's no more plan to it than there is to the course of the wind.

WEAVER: Yet, I believe that somehow—

DAVIS (*impatiently*): Somehow! Somehow! That's the trouble with you fellows. I've never known one of you who didn't work that word "somehow" overtime. You get up to a certain point; then you begin to "somehow." That word is the key to your chamber of mysteries; when reason and proof and intelligent method fail you, you drag in "somehow."

WEAVER: You would make of life a bitter thing. If our finer faith is an illusion, it is an illusion I would choose to keep. If life itself is illusion, I will make it a fine one rather than an ugly one.

DAVIS: Do you mean to say if a proof to the contrary were offered you, you would disregard the reality for a shadow? If a visible proof of what I am saying should walk through that door now would you persist in disregarding it?

WEAVER: I can imagine no proof sufficient to overthrow my belief. If men suffer, it is for some good purpose. The end is not pain. Life is beneficent.

DAVIS: That is the big error in your calculations. Why should life be beneficent? In fact, why should it take any great amount of interest in our doings? You are a frightful egoist if you imagine you are the pivot of the universe. You would make this great mysterious source which produced you more in sympathy with all your yearnings, throb with all your pains, show concern for all you think and feel and do. Yet that is no more reasonable than to suppose the spawning ground of minnows grows lonely for the hordes it belches out into the running stream. Do you suppose the mountain groans each time it gives birth to a mouse?

WEAVER: Yes, sir. I have courage enough to believe that.

DAVIS (*mimicking his tone*): Is that so, sir? Then you need courage enough not to believe it. The Process only asks that it be served and it does not care who serves it . . . Life. Life! We can no more control it than we can chain the winds. And what vessels we are to carry it. A poor wretched bundle of pains and aches and stealthy decay, still rudimentary and unfinished; living in ignorance or superstition.

WEAVER: Some day we shall rule over the stars.

DAVIS: Some day a swift and merciful plague will come, and erase us.

WEAVER: You should read the Book of Job again. God told Satan to afflict Man, to try to break his spirit, but to spare his life. For His spirit is in that life. It is divine and eternal.

DAVIS: I didn't know you were religious.

WEAVER: If we're moving in darkness, it is toward a light. In that all men may find comfort.

DAVIS: Did you ever see the light?

WEAVER: Most of us see it once. I have hopes of you yet, doctor.

DAVIS: Oh, I'm unregenerate. And my mental eyesight is normal. Dick, be sensible. You have made a blunder by coming here, a blunder that may turn out tragically. You're wasting yourself. You've offered yourself up as a sacrifice at the altar of youthful inexperience and idealism. Already I believe you're coming to see your mistake. Why be stubborn? You have much for the world; the world has much for you. Come with me.

WEAVER (*firmly*): You can't persuade me. My place is here. These people are ignorant, terribly ignorant, but I am one of them. I can't desert them now. Don't you realize what it means to me? When I was a boy I saw their life, the squalor, the ignorance, the poverty. When I went away, I knew I should come back.

DAVIS: That was a mistake. No young man should determine his life like that.

WEAVER: All my training, all those years of preparation were consecrated and made sacred by the thought that I was preparing myself for a ministry here.

DAVIS: Let me finish the picture for you. Do you dare to look ahead? The world is going by you outside these hills; it goes by you twice a day when the trains come in. If you stay you are lost, lost! Now you are young and capable. But in fifteen, twenty, twenty-five years! What then? You will go on with your patchwork here, giving pills, pulling babies, mending, sewing. And what is the end? A beefy country doctor with a broken-winded horse to haul you around! You are forgotten. Your science moves ahead but you are left behind.

WEAVER: Some one must do the patch-work. Some one must do the mending.

DAVIS: Then let some one do it. You can be a great man in your profession. But you must get away from here. There are hundreds of honest workmen coming from the medical schools each year who can do this kind of thing. But there's a touch of genius in you. You're wasting your talent here.

WEAVER: These are my people—my people!

DAVIS: The more reason you should leave them. I have watched them. They look on you already as a possession. How do you expect to maintain yourself in such an atmosphere?

WEAVER: I can't leave them now. I have seen too much. Even when I was away, I could never get the picture from my mind.

DAVIS: This is all very well as far as you're concerned. But have you thought of your wife, or your two children? The days are long and lonely when you're away in the mountains. Don't you suppose it's hard on her back here? There's no one she can talk to; you have taken her away from the things she has grown accustomed to.

WEAVER: We have been happy here. She would tell you so.

DAVIS: She has endured a great deal because she loves you, Dick. But, in your passion to help mankind, don't grow forgetful of those close to you. You have no right to check the growth of a human being. A man that does that has a great deal to answer for.

WEAVER: Do you think I have done that to my wife?

DAVIS: You must settle that for yourself. And you must remember that your children will soon begin their education. It is hard to look beyond the mountains.

WEAVER: Oh, when you come at me like that! Do you call it fair?

(*There is a brief pause. He continues slowly and quietly, after a moment.*)

Pardon me. You are quite right. The argument is fair.

DAVIS: There is another matter. I've heard a wild story about a quarrel between your people and some other mountain family. How much of it is true?

WEAVER: Oh, they're like a bunch of children with their quarrels, you know. (*Seriously.*) Only they remember them longer than children do. It doesn't really amount to much now, although it used to. About fifteen years ago my grandfather was killed by a man named Gudger in a dispute over a boundary line. My brother Tom, who was only a small boy then, saw the thing. For several years after there was very bitter feeling between the two factions which led to several fights. However, it has almost died down now, I believe. There has been no sign of trouble for years.

DAVIS: Then this thing happened within your time?

WEAVER: Oh, yes. I remember it quite well. I was a boy of fifteen or sixteen years.

DAVIS (*bluntly*): Did you ever take an active part in that quarrel?

WEAVER (*after a brief pause*): Yes, sir. I'm sorry to say I did. When I was seventeen, just before I went away, I went to a Hallowe'en party at a neighbor's. My father, who was then alive, had driven over to the place with Tom and me. Several of my relatives were there as well. The Gudger boys were there and two of them had been drinking. Trouble under those conditions was inevitable. One of them had a row with a cousin of mine and drew a knife. I was young and hot-blooded then, and I struck the fellow. His brother pulled out a gun and shot at me and wounded my cousin Jim Patton in the shoulder. He was overpowered and that ended it —for a while. Later, while I was away, trouble broke out again and one of the Gudgers was killed.

DAVIS: Did you ever tell Laura of this?

WEAVER: No. I knew it would worry her. And why dig up the Dark Ages? Those days are gone for me.

DAVIS (*regarding him curiously*): Are they?

WEAVER (*sharply*): Why do you say that?

DAVIS: Even now, Dick, are you sure? I have seen the temper of you people here. You are a hot-blooded race. Your training, you think, has somehow changed you. I wonder if it is really able to change you in so fundamental a way. Even now, are you sure you would be able to resist the call of your clan—and that's a strong call, Dick—if they were hard pressed and needed you?

WEAVER: Why, that's ridiculous. Do you mean to say I could revert to gun-toting, to animalism, to the level of the killer, after the training I've had?

DAVIS: It takes years to acquire such a training, but, often, the work of a moment will smash it down.

WEAVER: That is cheerful news. But the thing you speak of is impossible. I stand on the other side of an unbridged gap. I can talk to my people but never again can I walk with them. We are all players in a tragedy here—I, as well as the poorest farmer—but to me alone is it given to be a spectator as well.

DAVIS: You are too sure.

(*There is a rapping, feeble and hesitant, at the outer door. Mrs.*

Weaver passes through the hall and opens the door. Bessie, who has returned with her baby, enters.)

MRS. WEAVER: She wants to see you, Dick.

WEAVER: Sit down, Bessie.

(*The woman finds a chair.*)

DAVIS: I'll take a last look at the children before I go. Think about what I said.

(*Weaver nods.*)

MRS. WEAVER: They're not asleep yet. They've asked for you.

(*They go out. Weaver turns his attention to the woman. His manner is brusque; in the conversation that follows his voice has a harsh, at times a brutal, note.*)

WEAVER: Well, Bessie, what's the trouble?

BESSIE (*in even expressionless tones*): The baby's ailin' agin.

(*Weaver goes over and peers down at the child's face. He immediately shows anger.*)

WEAVER: What've you done to that child? He's starved, simply starved.

(*The woman makes no answer but regards him sullenly.*)

Haven't you been eating? What's become of all the food the neighbors sent in while you were in bed?

BESSIE: I don't want none o' no one's second-hand vittles.

WEAVER: Oh, you don't, eh? And how do you expect to live? I told you that child needed food. Why haven't you fed him?

BESSIE: I'll take none o' their leavin's.

WEAVER: Pride, pride! Do you know how God punishes people with pride like yours? He roasts them in the hottest corner of Hell.

(*She flinches, but remains defiant.*)

You don't deserve to have a baby, Bessie. Do you want to lose that child?

(*She holds the ragged bundle a little tighter.*)

BESSIE: I c'n git along without'n their charity, I reckon.

WEAVER: Yes. It looks like it. I've a notion to get that baby away from you, Bessie, and have him sent to the orphanage. There, at least, he'd get decent food.

(*She regards him steadily.*)

You don't believe I'd do that, eh?

BESSIE (*with quiet conviction*): No, ye wouldn't do that, doc.

WEAVER: And why not? I'd be well within my rights. No one would blame me. You've been no mother to that child. (*She winces.*) Oh, it may hurt, but it's the truth. Now, why shouldn't I take him away from you?

BESSIE: He's mine.

(*Suddenly she begins to sob in a dry and gasping manner, terrible to hear.*)

He's mine. You wouldn't do that, doc?

(*He becomes very tender and strokes her gently on her bent shoulders.*)

WEAVER: No, no. Don't worry. I couldn't do that. He's yours. No one will take him from you. But why will you starve the thing you love, Bessie? You are proud. What of that? I tell you if you had to crawl on your hands and knees from door to door begging food, you ought to get it for that baby.

(*Nothing can be heard for a moment save the woman's racking sobs.*)

Where is your beast of a husband? Out on a spree, I suppose.

BESSIE: I don't know an' I don't care. I ain't seen nor heerd tell of him come six weeks.

WEAVER: Why do you put up with that fellow? He gives you no money, does he?

BESSIE: No, an' I don't want nothin' of his'n.

WEAVER: He gets enough money from the rotten, cheap

whiskey he's selling. What if I should tell you he's fooling with another woman?

(*She moves convulsively.*)

BESSIE: Hit ain't so! (*Fiercely.*) Ef he's goin' with her agin, I'll kill him. She's nothin' but a common chippy, an' everyone knows hit.

WEAVER: Then there is another woman?

BESSIE: You don't know nothin'?

(*She relapses into sullen silence.*)

WEAVER: Now, see here, Bessie, I can't help you or your baby unless you obey me. The child needs food. It does you no good to bring him to me unless you feed him. If you won't let other people help you, you'll have to go to work and help yourself. What was the trouble with you and Mrs. Sam Bartlett? I thought you started to work there.

BESSIE: I wan't goin' to put up fer her high-an'-mighty airs. I wan't goin' to slave while she was layin' in bed or flyin' aroun' makin' calls.

WEAVER: Then, good heavens, what do you intend to do? You can't expect to dictate to the people you work for. I give you fair warning: You'll lose that child if you don't take better care of him.

BESSIE: We'll git along somehow, I reckon.

WEAVER: Somehow! Somehow!

(*He pauses, startled by the repetition of the word. He continues persuasively:*)

Bessie, will you let me help you? I'll look after you until you and the baby are strong again. Then you can go to work.

BESSIE: Yeah, I'll let you help me. But I don't want none o' their charity. They'd go on forever about hit.

(*Weaver gives the woman money from his purse. She takes it silently and thrusts it into the bosom of her dress.*)

WEAVER: Go home and rest. And feed yourself. Food for

you is food for the baby. You understand. (*She nods*) Don't worry about the money. You can pay me when you find work.

(*She starts to go but pauses and returns to him.*)

BESSIE: I reckon ye're right. I oughtn't to have a baby. I'm sorry I had him.

WEAVER: Surely, you don't mean that, Bessie?

BESSIE: Yeah. Hit would've been better all 'round. But I've got him now an' I'm goin' to keep him. They ain't goin' to take him from me, air they?

WEAVER (*gently*): No, Bessie. He's yours. They can't take him from you.

BESSIE: I got some pride left, I reckon.

(*Weaver makes a gesture of amused despair.*)

Well I ain't goin' to have no one say to my boy when he's growed up that his mother fed him off'n charity.

WEAVER: Yes. I understand.

(*He looks down at the little bundle and prods it gently with his finger.*)

Smile. That's the boy. He never cries, does he, Bessie?

BESSIE: No. He don't never make no noise.

WEAVER: What big eyes you have, Buster! He keeps that mouth clamped tight, doesn't he? There's only one way to loosen him up, Bessie. Give him food. (*Speaking to the child.*) When you come back here again, I want to see you fat. D'you understand that? I want a little round pot here. (*He prods the child's stomach.*) That makes you laugh, doesn't it? (*To the woman.*) It wouldn't hurt him if he made a little more noise, Bessie.

BESSIE: Oh, he's a quiet young un. He never cries. We'll git along, doc.

(*She starts to go. Davis and Mrs. Weaver return.*)

MRS. WEAVER: A dear little baby! Won't you let me see him, please? There you are!

(*Smiling she looks down into the child's face. Immediately, however, her face shows horror; she gives an involuntary exclamation, and draws back, becoming pale and quiet. Davis, who has come up behind her and looked, becomes grave. Bessie, sullen and defiant, goes out slowly.*)

How terrible! I'm sorry I looked.

DAVIS: It is always dangerous to look, my dear. Remember the sad fate of the Lady of Shalott. (*With a tinge of irony he speaks to Weaver.*) Well, Richard, shall we go now?

WEAVER (*slowly and painfully*): That was an extreme case.

DAVIS: Exactly! It takes an extreme case sometimes to prove our point!

MRS. WEAVER: That poor child. He looked like a little old man.

DAVIS (*with scientific imperturbability*): It's very strange how old an underfed child can look. (*Briskly.*) Well, Dick, are you going to the train with me?

WEAVER: Yes, of course. Where are your bags?

DAVIS: In the hall. (*He turns to his daughter to take his leave.*) Well, my dear, this is the hardest part of all.

(*Weaver has gone into the hall.*)

MRS. WEAVER: Won't you stay over until tomorrow, father?

DAVIS: No. I must go now. I've eaten the lotus long enough. They're calling for me.

(*The train whistle blows very near. He starts hurriedly.*) Good gracious, I must run. (*He embraces her quickly.*) You must talk to him, Laura. See what you can do. I've done my best. I think he's coming over. It's telling on him here. He's not so sure now. Goodbye, dear. (*He kisses her again.*) Won't you go to the train with me?

MRS. WEAVER (*dabbing her eyes*): No, father, I'm afraid I couldn't bear it. But I'll stand in the window and wave to you when the train goes by.

WEAVER (*calling from the hall*): You'd better hurry, father. Your train's almost here.

(*Davis departs quickly. The outer door opens and closes. Very near at hand now the whistle sounds, and the pounding of the heavy train wheels may be heard. Mag enters wearing a sunbonnet.*)

MRS. WEAVER: Tom hasn't come yet?

MAG: No, ma'am. But, then, I cal'c'lated on his being late.

MRS. WEAVER: You and Tom have been going together a long time, haven't you, Mag?

MAG: Yes'm. I reckon Tom means business, shore.

MRS. WEAVER: Oh! Then he's spoken to you?

MAG: Well, not in so many words. But ye c'n allus tell, cain't ye?

MRS. WEAVER (*beginning to laugh*): Well! Yes, I suppose you can.

(*The train comes in at the station below.*)

There's the train! (*Peering out the window.*) Yes, they're going to make it all right. There's father, now. He's getting on.

MAG: Yore paw lives a right smart ways off, don't he?

MRS. WEAVER: Yes. Very far, Mag.

MAG: I'd like to take a trip like that—off on the cyars, I mean. I guess hit's purty seein' things like that.

MRS. WEAVER: Maybe, if all goes well, you and Tom will make a wedding trip.

MAG: No'm. I reckon not. I'd jest go home with him.

(*The whistle blows, the bell clangs, the train starts.*)

MRS. WEAVER (*crying excitedly*): Goodbye, father. Goodbye! (*Waving her handkerchief violently and crying.*) Goodbye! Goodbye!

MAG: What air ye goin' on like that fer? He cain't hear ye.

(*A long row of lights flash by the window and the train has gone. Mrs. Weaver comes slowly and thoughtfully back to the center of the room.*)

MRS. WEAVER: No. I suppose not. But, then, he could see me in the window. He saw me wave! Dear father!

(*The sound of the train recedes rapidly and one immediately becomes conscious of the great silence of the night; a silence broken only by the mixed harmony of the night sounds, rising and falling in a peaceful monotone, for summer has not yet entirely gone.)*

How quiet it becomes. The train rushes in, and the lights go by, and then we are left alone again.

MAG: Alone? I reckon not.

MRS. WEAVER: You don't understand that, do you, Mag? When the train comes I am not lonely. Then it goes, and everything is different. It's queer, isn't it? The world comes in just twice a day—and goes out twice a day. See who's at the door, Mag.

(Mag goes to the door and returns accompanied by Tom Weaver, a young mountaineer in the early twenties. He is shy, reserved, and laconic in his speech until suddenly aroused, when he displays primitive and uncontrollable passions.)

Good evening, Tom. You are late.

TOM: Yes'm. Whar's brother Dick?

MRS. WEAVER: He went to the train with father. He should be back now.

TOM: Oh! Yore paw's gone, has he?

MRS. WEAVER: Yes. He couldn't stay any longer.

(Weaver returns.)

WEAVER: Good evening, Tom.

TOM: Evenin', Dick.

WEAVER: You've been a stranger lately.

TOM: I'm gettin' my place in order.

WEAVER: Well, that's fine. All you need now is a housekeeper.

TOM *(with a sidelong glance at Mag)*: I'm figgerin' on that, too.

(She blushes and giggles.)

Well, I reckon we'll be gittin' on, Mag.

WEAVER: You are going so soon? I had hoped you'd stay to supper.

TOM: No, I reckon not. Thankee.

(*He starts to go, but returns, addresses his brother, at first with some awkwardness, but with considerable earnestness as he goes on.*)

Dick, I heerd t'other day ye're tradin' at Gudger's sto'.

WEAVER: Of course. We have an account there. (*Sharply.*) What are you driving at, Tom?

TOM: Oh, nothin'. Only I wouldn't if I was you. Folks is talkin' 'bout hit.

WEAVER: And what's so strange about it? It's the only decent store in the village.

TOM: Folks air sayin' hit looks mighty queer when a Weaver starts doin' business with a Gudger.

WEAVER: Well, there's nothing strange about it and folks can say what they please. I'll trade wherever I want to.

TOM: I wouldn't talk like that whar folks c'd hear me, Dick. Yore folks might not like hit.

WEAVER (*angrily*): Well, the sooner they get used to it, the better. I'm not going to be fenced in by that foolish old quarrel. It's time we were forgetting it.

TOM: Mebbe. Mebbe. But yore folks don't look at hit like you do. (*A pause.*) The fac' is, they're askin' what ye're goin' to do?

WEAVER: What I'm going to do? What do you mean?

TOM: Ef thar's trouble with that gang folks want to know what side o' the fence ye're standin' on.

WEAVER (*violently*): Good God, man, what are you talking about? Do you think I'm going to take any part in your silly row?

MRS. WEAVER (*interposing quickly*): Don't you think, Tom, some other time would be better to talk about this thing? The doctor is very tired tonight.

TOM: Oh, all right, ma'am. I didn't go to rile you, Dick. Only we don't know about things or when they'll happen. I ain't forcin' ye. No one wants to do that. We know ye'll do the right thing by yore folks when the time comes. But I wouldn't go makin' frien's with that gang, ef I was you. Hit don't look right.

WEAVER: I'm a practicing physician and I have no time for a family quarrel. I'm not a schoolboy any longer. They can't dictate to me.

TOM (*in an aggrieved voice*): Lord! Who's tryin' to? We know ye're with us, Dick. (*Nodding wisely to Mrs. Weaver.*) He's all right. When we was boys together—

WEAVER (*impatiently*): Oh, but it's different with us now, Tom—You and I. Don't you see?

TOM: You mean we ain't boys no more?

(*Weaver makes an impatient gesture.*)

Well, that's so, ain't it? No offense, Dick. I know ye'll allus do the right thing. Well, I reckon we'll git along.

(*He goes out with Mag. Weaver, somewhat agitated, walks around nervously. The door opens and shuts outside and he makes a movement as if to recall his brother. Mrs. Weaver restrains him.*)

MRS. WEAVER: I wouldn't say anything to him just now, Dick. You're dreadfully upset. Why must you let these things annoy you so?

WEAVER: Oh, that air of possession! It drives me mad when one of them adopts that attitude. I want them to know once and for all that I've outgrown all that foolishness. It seems they would have sense enough to know. But just as soon as I came back here, they began to treat me as if nothing had happened. Just as if I was the same ignorant mountain boy who went away.

MRS. WEAVER: You must be patient with them, Richard. They don't understand.

WEAVER: No? Well, I'll drive it through the thickness of their skulls once and for all. If trouble should break out, I suppose they'd expect me to tote a gun with the rest of them. (*He laughs harshly.*) What a farce!

MRS. WEAVER (*quietly*): You have a hot temper. They're nothing but great, big children and you can't afford to antagonize them.

WEAVER: They shan't control me! They shan't! (*Suddenly.*) Good Lord, but I'm tired. (*He sinks heavily into a chair.*) The first of the week! Just think of it. And I'm already tired. Sic transit a glorious Monday!

MRS. WEAVER (*impulsively*): Richard, I—

(*She pauses. He takes her hand across the table.*)

WEAVER: What, dear?

MRS. WEAVER: Did father talk to you?

WEAVER: Yes.

(*There is another, more protracted pause.*)

You want to go back?

(*She answers in a low, scarcely audible voice which trembles.*)

MRS. WEAVER: You must decide. I won't—I couldn't bear to force you.

WEAVER (*steadily*): And do you think I would put anything in the world before you? You must know I wouldn't.

(*She comes swiftly around the table and sits on the arm of his chair.*)

MRS. WEAVER: It is not for me, but for yourself that you must decide. I've spent sleepless nights watching and wondering about you. Dick! Dick! Is it worth it all—the hardship, the discouragement, the loneliness?

WEAVER (*after a searching glance*): What do you think?

(*The whistle blows from the mountain side. She starts.*)

MRS. WEAVER: Do you hear that? Father's on that train.

WEAVER: You will miss him now.

MRS. WEAVER: Yes. It will be hard for a time. But, then, we can't keep him always.

WEAVER: Five years! Five years! It seems longer than that, doesn't it, dear?

MRS. WEAVER: Yes. It has been long.

WEAVER: Do you remember that spring when we first came here?

MRS. WEAVER: The mountains were beautiful then.

WEAVER: Yes. They were beautiful—then. We went off and

made our camp on Bald Pate—just you and I. How long did we stay there? Do you remember?

MRS. WEAVER: Three days. Had you forgotten?

WEAVER: Yes. That is right. Three days. There was a lot of laurel and rhododendron that year. The mountains were covered with it.

MRS. WEAVER: It was glorious.

WEAVER: Five years! (*After a brief pause.*) Do you remember that fellow in the Bible who said, "Lord, I am here." And he was answered.

(*He smiles, but there is a note of despair in his voice.*)

I have called out every day and every night, "I am here, here!" but it seems to fail.

(*She presses him on the arm.*)

MRS. WEAVER: Don't.

(*There is a pause.*)

Oh, I believe it will come out all right if we are patient.

WEAVER: Patient. "There was a man named Job who lived in the land of Uz." It sometimes seems his descendants people the earth. When your father talked to me tonight, my doubts came back. After all, I am only a young man and all I have is my faith. But he was so sure; he knew what he knew so well. And he is deep, your father. He carries weight.

MRS. WEAVER: My dear, if faith is all you have, it is enough. You mustn't lose that now. It has kept you strong and fine. And— we've got to believe in something. I know how wise father talks. But down beneath even he has his belief.

WEAVER: It is so hard, so hard. (*There is a pause.*) Perhaps he was right. He was right about you, at any rate, and the children.

MRS. WEAVER (*quickly*): What did he say?

WEAVER: It was true. I had no right to bring you here—a girl like you. I've kept you in prison for five years.

MRS. WEAVER: You haven't.

WEAVER: Yes, he was right. It must have been hell for you. The loneliness and the waiting—while I was away.

MRS. WEAVER: No, there were the children.

WEAVER: It's strange how we can forget. I lost myself in my work. I've almost grown old in five years. That spring—when we came—I'd almost forgotten that too. And that spring was the best of all. All that we knew was that the air was sweet and the sun was warm. And it's enough, if we know that.

MRS. WEAVER: No. That's not enough.

WEAVER: You think not?

MRS. WEAVER: A woman learns that the things we love are purchased in pain. Things that are true and fine must be bought with suffering. They must have their birth-pangs.

WEAVER: And is the game worth the candle? No. He was right. When spring comes again, we will go.

MRS. WEAVER: Go—away?

WEAVER: Yes. Away from the mountains—the beautiful and terrible mountains, who crush people under their weight.

(*The whistle blows faintly.*)

And we will get a new set of gods. The old ones have treated us badly. Perhaps they were false.

MRS. WEAVER: No, no, Dick. You mustn't talk that way. You shan't go now.

WEAVER: You are a strange woman. You wanted to go above all things; now you would stay.

MRS. WEAVER: I want to keep you as you are. That is all that matters. I couldn't bear to see you change.

WEAVER: But you can't keep me as I am. I've changed already—in five years. Everything is bound to change—people most of all. What is there that doesn't change? Except the mountains. What man is the same one spring as he was the last?

MRS. WEAVER: Men grow stronger and greater.

WEAVER: Man is a proud, swift being capable of moving mountains. Then he decays and is senile and weak and old. We grow strong to sicken and die. When we think we're learning to live, we're learning to die. That is the process of growth. And the mountains remain. They can't grow at all; they can't add even an inch to their stature. There's something splendid about that.

They're secure in their strength. Eternal, changeless mountains. The victory is ultimately yours. If winter comes, the spring will always bring you youth again. So, like the gods, they grow old only to be young again.

MRS. WEAVER: Why do you speak of them like that? As if they were alive?

WEAVER: And who can say that they are not—in every respect, save that of motion. And I, who have lived beneath them, have seen them move. I have seen them send a crushing slide down on the little farmer's land. I have seen them pour their water on his crops and drown them. I have seen them hold the people in their grip, keeping them within their limits, holding them in an awful spell, yielding them a half-living from their stony soil, choosing to kill them slowly.

MRS. WEAVER: Dick, Dick. You mustn't talk like that. You frighten me!

WEAVER (*after a pause*): No. It's not worth it. It's a deadly, inevitable strugle. And I can't prevail. In the spring we will go. If it's a matter of getting and spending, we'll get and spend.

(*The door is thrown open outside without the preliminary of a knock and Bessie, the mountain woman, rushes in. There is wild fear in her manner. She bears the child in her arm.*)

BESSIE: Doc. What's wrong with my baby? Look at him! He won't speak!

(*Weaver looks. He takes the still bundle, puts his head against the child's face, and silently draws a corner of the blanket up over its head. He restores the bundle to the mother.*)

WEAVER: He didn't make any sound?
BESSIE: I didn't hear nothin', Doc!
WEAVER (*gently*): Go home, Bessie. I can't help you now. You've lost your baby.

(*The woman stands stupidly, hardly comprehending what he is saying.*)

MRS. WEAVER: Oh, the poor thing! Can't we do something to help you?

BESSIE: No. (*With smouldering anger in her voice.*) I don't want no one's charity, no one's. He didn't make no noise. I never knowed nothin', he was so quiet. If he'd only made a noise. Me a-sittin' thar an' holdin' him, an' he didn't make no noise. (*Fiercely.*) I wan't goin' to take their charity to feed 'im. I got some pride.

(*Mrs. Weaver moves toward the woman, but Weaver warns her away. Bessie goes out. It seems much darker within the room. The lamp on the table is wholly insufficient to combat the darkness. The Night that surrounds the house is impenetrable and black. Weaver stands shades in semi-darkness looking out of the window.*)

WEAVER: Did you ever see a darker night? You should have seen his face! The mouth was closed tighter than ever. He made no noise, she said. He was a good soldier. He had—courage. That's a big thing.

(*He turns to her impulsively and draws her to him.*)

You wouldn't leave me! You wouldn't leave me now!

MRS. WEAVER: Leave you? But if you stay, I stay, of course. (*Suddenly she cries out as if wounded.*) Oh, why did you say that?

(*Below, far in the distance, the train rushes out of the mountains. The pounding of its wheels can be faintly heard and its ghostly whistle floats back from some moonlit plain. They listen.*)

MRS. WEAVER (*presently, in quiet, matter-of-fact tones*): Don't you think you'd better go to bed? You are tired. And tomorrow is a long day.

CURTAIN

ACT II

SETTING: *Tom Weaver's home. The scene is a large, untidy room which is used by the family for eating, sleeping and the preparation of food. From time to time as Tom Weaver made his painful advance in the world he added to his domicile in the way he thought justified by his increased dignity of position. Thus, this room which was once all in all his home has been augmented by another room of like proportions tacked onto the left like a soapbox and a lean-to kitchen shed which runs off from the back. There are openings at the back and left to these rooms and a door at the right to the outside. The walls are of logs chinked with mud and heavily blackened by years of smoke most of which does not go up the chimney. The hearth and chimney, wide, spacious and draughty, is at the left where it can do double service to both rooms.*

There is a small window high up to the right of the opening at the back; this gives the room its only illumination. There is a couch with a checkered quilt under the window, a rude table with an oil cloth cover and four chairs around it, in the centre, a rifle on wood forks over the hearth, a wooden clock on the mantel, a dilapidated cupboard next the door at the back and various lithographs of religious nature on the walls.

One in particular catches the eye. It is a representation of Our Lord seated on a cloud, surrounded by a legion of white and black angels and black and white cherubs. The inscription reads: "God loves them both." Tom bought this from a negro man when he made a peddling expedition to a town in the foothills.

There are the red embers of a fire in the hearth and an iron pot sits boiling on them.

At first the room is empty. Then Sam, Tom Weaver's youngest son, comes in through the door at the right. He is carrying an armful of wood which he dumps heavily on the hearth. He stands slapping his hands free of dust. Sam is a good-looking boy of sixteen with a tough, lean physique. He has a keen, intelligent face and sombre, smouldering eyes.

He kicks two or three vagrant sticks over on the pile on the hearth and, going back, nearly slams the door in the face of his father who enters with an armful of harness which he throws on the floor.

> TOM (*angrily*): Mind what ye're doin'!
> SAM (*sullenly*): I didn't see ye.
> TOM: Where's yore maw?

SAM (*nodding toward the shed*): Out thar I reckon.

TOM: Did ye git in the wood? (*Sam nods.*) Done the milkin'?

SAM: No I hain't. Hit's Reese's turn.

TOM: You let Reese be. He can take keer of himse'f. I sent him to town to git some victuals.

SAM: Whyn't ye let me go? He went last time.

TOM: None of yore business. Ye like to go to town too damn good anyway. Last time I sent ye, ye was gone all day. Ye're gittin' too many fool notions in yore head as hit is.

SAM (*sullenly*): You knowed cousin Dick was goin' off today. Looks like ye might've let me go. Hit's my last chanct to see him.

TOM (*ironically*): Ain't that too bad, now? I suppose hit'll break Dick's heart not to see ye agin.

SAM (*truculently*): We been good friends.

TOM: Oh ye have, have ye? I s'pose ye think yore cousin Dick's in love with ye because ye've been huntin with him a few times. (*Roughly.*) Ain't ye got no sense? He's taken ye with him because he wanted someone to talk to.

SAM (*his pride touched*): Hit ain't so. He likes me.

TOM: Goin' in to yore uncle's house a few times has turned yore head. What use have them folks fer the like of you! Now go on out and tend to yore milkin' without no more argyin'.

(*Sam scowling darkly picks up a pail and starts for the door. His brother Reese, a heavy looking lout of eighteen years, comes in and deposits a market basket on the table. Tom eyes him suspiciously.*)

Have ye enjoyed yore vacation? Ye've been gone long enough.

REESE (*surlily*): I wan't gone no longer than I could help. Hit's drizzlin' rain anyway.

SAM (*coming back and putting the pail in his brother's hand*): Hit's yore turn today. I hain't goin' to do yore milkin' all the time.

REESE: What d'ye take me fer? D'ye think I'm going to town an' do the milkin' to boot? (*Puts the pail on the table with a bang and walks off.*)

SAM (*stubbornly*): I'd a gone to town ef they'd let me. Hit was my turn anyway.

REESE: Mad because ye couldn't go in an' see yore dere, sweet, little Dick, ain't ye?

SAM: You shet up! Ef ye'd been any 'count ye wouldn't have beat me out of goin'. I let you go last time.

REESE: Well, I ain't goin' to do no milkin'. Git out o' my way!

(*He gives Sam a shove. Sam picks up a stick of wood and advances threateningly.*)

SAM: I'll lam ye one with this stick of wood ef ye don't do that milkin'.

REESE: Let's see ye!

(*Tom, who has been going over the harness, comes in quickly between the two.*)

TOM: We ain't goin' to have no rowin'. Both of ye shet up or I'll cowhide ye. (*Wrenches stick from Sam's hand.*) A purty thing ye air to be layin' in to yore brother!

REESE: That's right, paw. He ain't got no call to go jumpin' on me. I never done nuthin' to him.

TOM: You be quiet too. He's right. Hit's yore turn to do the milkin' an' I want to see ye do hit without no more whinin'. (*He gives the unwilling boy a shove.*) Stop yore sulkin', Sam, or I'll give ye something to sulk over.

REESE (*going*): Ye'd better ask him what he was doin' down the road t'other day with Clem Gudger and his sister Mary.

TOM: What's this?

SAM: You tend to yore business, Reese, an' I'll tend to mine.

REESE: Yeah, him an' Dick Weaver, too. The hull crowd was walkin' along together as thick as thieves.

SAM: Ye damn sneak! I'll git even fer this.

TOM: You, Reese, git out and tend to yore milk. (*Reese goes. Tom turns menacingly to Sam.*) Now, what's this all about? Have ye been goin' with any of that crowd? (*Sam doesn't answer.*) Have ye?

SAM: Well what ef I have? I don't see as how we done no harm.

TOM (*dangerously quiet*): Oh, ye don't. An' when did all this happen?

SAM: T'other day. Dick un me was walkin' along comin' from the sto' an' Clem an' Mary come by. They spoke to us jest as nice as ye please an' Dick spoke back at em an' we kinder went on a little an' stopped an' looked back an' so did they an' then we talked a little mo' an' walked back an' they walked up an' purty soon we was all talkin' an' goin' along together.

TOM: Tryin' to put hit off on Dick, air ye?

SAM (*like a flash*): No I hain't. Thar ain't nothin' to put off noway. I ain't done nothin' to be skeered of.

TOM: Well, we'll jest see about that. Mebbe by the time I git done with ye, ye won't be so spunky about hit.

(*He stands looking at the boy a moment and his wrath explodes. He gives him a cuff that sends him spinning back half a dozen feet to fall across the table.*)

I'll larn ye to go meddlin' with that gang. (*Advancing.*) Air ye goin' to do hit agin?

SAM (*getting up wild with rage*): I'll do hit now when I damn please an' ye hain't goin' to keep me from hit.

TOM (*quickly*): I'm goin' to give ye a lesson ye're not apt to fergit.

(*Seizes him; Mag enters from the shed.*)

MAG: You leave him alone, Tom Weaver. A nice one you air to go beatin' an' cuffin' yore own boy when he's wuked like a dawg fer ye.

TOM: He ain't goin' with that gang an' then give me back talk about hit.

MAG: Well, ye let go of him. (*Takes his hands and throws them off the boy's shoulders.*) I reckon I've got some say so an' I ain't goin' to see you abusin' him.

TOM: I might've knowed you'd honey him along. But I ain't goin' to stand fer no goin's on with them Gudgers an' the sooner he knows hit the better hit'll be fer him.

MAG: I don't see as he's done no crime. Hit's little enough fun he gits anyway. Dick was in hit just as much as he was.

TOM: Yeuh! An' I'll tell Dick's paw the fust chanct I git, too.

MAG: Ef ye want to know what I think, his paw wouldn't be sorry to see his boy make friends with the Gudgers.

TOM: Ah! Ye talk too much.

SAM (*moodily*): I don't git no fun out o' nuthin'. I got to stay aroun' heah all the time an' ef I speak to anyone I git layed out fer hit. I wisht I was dead.

TOM: That right. Hit's jest like ye to be wishin' ye were layin' down all the time, ye lazy dawg.

SAM: Looks like I might've gone in to see Dick today. I won't see him agin fer a long spell.

TOM: Air ye goin' to shet up about that? I'm tired hearin' your blubberin'.

MAG: Well why didn't ye let him go in to town? The boy's right. He does the wuk of two Reeses an' hit was his time to go.

TOM (*irritated*): I'll jest trouble you to keep yore mouth shet.

MAG: All right. I'll jest trouble you to git your own supper. When the time comes when I can't open my mouth after slavin' like a dawg all day fer ye I'll jest quit cookin'. (*She seats herself calmly and folds her hands.*)

TOM: I reckon when all's said an' done I do about as much wuk aroun' heah as you do. (*Grumbling.*) I never said he couldn't go, nohow, I never thought.

MAG: No. No one ud expect ye to.

(*There is the sound of sand and gravel and small stones sliding down somewhere outside. There is but a spurt and it is over. Tom looks startled, Mag looks at him accusingly. He hurries over to the window and gives a sigh of relief.*)

TOM: Hit ain't nuthin—jest a little dirt come rollin' down.

MAG: I thought ye said ye was goin' to fix that today.

TOM (*shortly*): I ain't had no time fer hit. I been at my plowin' an' Reese was gone. How d'ye expect me to tend to everythin'?

MAG: Ef hit rains tonight ye'll wisht ye had. That hull bank is ready to cave in on top of the shed. That's what ye git fer diggin' in yore house at the foot of a hill.

TOM: I had to git some pertection agin the weather, didn't I?

MAG: Yeah! An' we git hit don't we? Every time the rains come ye've got to putter yore time away keepin' the hill from movin' down on us.

TOM (*casting a practiced eye at the weather*): Hit ain't goin' to rain tonight. Hit's clearin' off.

MAG: That's another one of your prophecies that ain't likely to come true!

TOM: I'll git the boys the fust thing in the mornin' an' we'll drive the logs in an' stop hit.

MAG (*with growing bitterness*): Ye drove the logs in last year an' whar air they now? Hit went right on oveh them like they warn't there. An' when d'ye think hits goin' to stop? Hit's been movin' down on the house every rain come the last five years. No, ye hain't goin' to keep hit from movin'. Ef thar's any movin' bein' done we'll be the ones to do hit. I tell ye.

TOM (*uneasily*): Hit don't move but a few foot a year.

MAG: God! I wisht it would all come at onct an' git done with hit. Jest a settin' heah and waitin' while hit creeps down a few foot at a time is fair maddenin'.

TOM: Aw! Stop yore goin' on I got enough troubles without havin' to listen to yore groanin'.

(*A dog's barking is heard outside and the rattle of carriage wheels. Sam runs to the door and opens it.*)

SAM (*joyfully*): It's Dick!

(*Weaver followed by Richard comes in. Richard is staggering under the weight of four large calf-skin volumes which he deposits on table.*)

WEAVER: Good evening, Tom. How are you, Mag?

MAG: Didn't expect to see ye out heah today, Dick.

WEAVER: Dick decided he had to see Sam before he went, so we drove out.

TOM: How air ye, Dick?

RICHARD (*shortly*): All right, Uncle Tom. (*To Sam.*) I thought you said you were coming in today. (*Sam looks nervously at his father.*)

TOM: Oh, ye were goin' in today, were ye?

WEAVER: Hello, Sammy! What's the matter? You look as if you've lost your last friend.

SAM: Aw nuthin', Uncle Dick.

TOM: I've jest been givin' him a lesson he's been needin' a long time. (*Curiously.*) What've ye got thar, Dick?

RICHARD: Ridpath's *History of the World*, in four volumes. I'm giving them to Sam.

SAM: Dick! Air they fer me? (*Goes quickly to the table and opens a volume.*)

TOM (*roughly*): Aw, what's the use of that. He cain't read what's in 'em.

SAM (*humiliated*): I reckon I can learn ef I want to.

RICHARD: There's lots of pictures, Sam.

MAG: Ye leave him be, Tom. I reckon ef he wants 'em and Dick wants to give 'em to him, hit's nobody's business.

TOM: I don't know as I want him to have 'em.

SAM: Aw, paw!

TOM: Ye'd only putter time away ye might be puttin' in earnin' yore keep.

WEAVER: Sam's the largest beneficiary in Dick's will. Dick's leaving him his dog as well as numerous other possessions.

SAM: Air ye leavin' me Bob?

RICHARD: Not for good, understand. Just until I get back. You'll take good care of him, won't you, Sam? (*Sam nods, too moved to speak.*)

TOM: Dick, I hear as how ye've been makin' friends with Clem and Mary Gudger.

RICHARD (*in hurt surprise to Sam*): You told him!

SAM: I did not! Hit was that sneak of a Reese.

TOM (*to Weaver*): Have you heerd about this?

WEAVER (*unperturbed*): I can't say that I have. What's it all about?

TOM: Nothin' except that yore boy and my Sam was walkin' down the road with that Clem and Mary Gudger t'other day jest as nice an' sociable as ye please.

SAM: Aw, paw. What'd ye tell on him fer?

TOM: You keep quiet an' don't speak till ye're asked.

WEAVER: Mary's a pretty girl. I was noticing her just the other day. (*Calmly.*) In fact I picked her up and drove her home.

TOM (*incredulously*): You did?

WEAVER (*good humoredly*): Pshaw! Blame Dick, not me. I'll soon be old and I learned to like pretty girls young. You can't teach an old dog new tricks. But Dick—he's young enough to know better, isn't he? (*Puts his arm around the boy's shoulder.*)

TOM: I gave Sam a lesson he ain't likely to fergit.

RICHARD (*to his father*): I know you think I was making up to Mary, but I wasn't. They came by us on the road and were so nice and pleasant and everything that I didn't have the heart to act mean about it.

TOM (*angrily*): You look heah, Dick—

WEAVER: Just a minute—please! What would you have him do? You can't blame the boy for acting like a gentleman, can you?[1]

TOM: He ain't got no business meddlin' with that gang an' ye oughter tell him so.

RICHARD (*imperiously*): You're not going to boss me around, Uncle Tom. I'll go with who I please and you can't stop me.

WEAVER (*gently remonstrative*): Dick! Dick! Be more respectful.

RICHARD (*defiantly*): Well, he's not. When I come back, I bet I won't listen to him. How d'ye ever expect me to go anywhere or meet anyone? There's a Hallowe'en party at the schoolhouse. I can't go. Uncle Tom says the Gudgers will be there. I get invited out to Bishop's on New Year's. I can't go. Uncle Tom says there'll be Gudgers there. I reckon if I die and go to heaven Uncle Tom won't let me in if there are any Gudgers there.

TOM (*grimly*): Ye needn't worry, thar won't be.

WEAVER: Pshaw! No doubt heaven's full of people just as good as the Gudgers. (*Tom fumes.*)

RICHARD (*with unthinking boylike brutality*): Well, all I've got to say is, if I go off and come back here when I'm a doctor I don't want to have to do like you've done, pa.

WEAVER (*quietly*): What do you mean, son?

1. This sentence added to typescript in pencil.

RICHARD: I want to be friends with everyone. I want to go and see them all if they're sick and need me.

WEAVER: I always go to see people when they need me, Dick.

RICHARD: No you don't, Pa. You go if they send for you but there are lots of people who won't send for you. Old bow-legged Gudger let his wife 'most die because he wouldn't call you in. (*Weaver winces. Richard addresses himself to Sam.*) Where you going to keep that dawg, Sam?

SAM: In the barn. I reckon, till I get a place fixed fer him.

RICHARD: Well, show me where you're going to put him. I want to know you're taking good care of him. (*They go out.*)

WEAVER: Well, he hit me there, Tom.

TOM: If he was my youngun I'd teach him to hold his tongue.

WEAVER: For telling the truth? (*There is a pause; Weaver proceeds with quiet earnestness.*) No, the boy is right; as a matter of fact, why keep the old sores open? There's been no trouble for years. I find myself forgetting about it at times and I believe the Gudgers are disposed to do the same thing.

TOM (*violently*): I ain't goin' to listen to no such talk, Dick.

WEAVER: But is it quite fair to these youngsters growing up around us to breed in them the same hate that was bred in us?

MAG: No hit hain't. My Sam don't like hit no mo' than yore Dick.

TOM: Oh—yore Sam!

WEAVER: My life has had a bitter flavor, Tom. Yet, I'm not a bitter man at heart.

TOM: Ye're too soft. Ye allus were. When I think o' that damn, bloody murderin' crew hit fair makes my blood bile. No, I won't evah make up to them an' ef a boy o' mine ud evah make up to 'em after I'm gone I'd come back from my grave an' curse him.

WEAVER: Tom! Tom! Why feed your heart out to your tongue!

TOM: I don't fergit, Dick. Thar ain't no use in trying. God! When I think of that day on the hill when they shot gran'paw! Hit all comes back again an' I can't fergit.

WEAVER: Perhaps I'd feel differently if I'd been there to see it. But Tom, it has been so long. Can't we have peace?

TOM: No!

WEAVER: I'm sending my boy away tonight. He'll be gone a long time. But when he comes back some day ready to go on with his life's work, I don't want him to have to go through the same mill his father has been through.

MAG: No, an' I don't blame you neither, Dick. Thar's enough trouble in the world without ahuntin' fer hit. (*She goes into the shed.*)

WEAVER: To continue this thing is madness. It's a disease, a crawling horror in the blood that has to be cut out. Consider what a hole it has knocked in our lives and to what end? You can't say, no more than I, let's stop it. When I say stop, I mean cut it short. Let's stop, with no gradual beginning, no coming over in time, but now.

TOM: No!

WEAVER: The only remedy is a surgical operation. Let's cut out our hate. Yesterday we were enemies with the Gudgers. Tomorrow we'll be friends.

TOM: Not while I'm livin'! Nor you neither, Dick. We're tarred with the same stick. Ye can't begin a thing like this an' watch hit goin' on year aftah year an' then stop hit. Ye begun yore life agin the Gudgers, ye'll end hit that-a-way. Yore boy's comin' heah to take yore work up whar ye leave hit off—

WEAVER: No! Not where I leave it off but where I begun!

TOM: Yore boy's comin' back to take hit up an' I hope to God his boy'll do the same.

WEAVER (*with a shudder*): No. No. I won't have that! He shan't be made to go through with it.

TOM: But he will, jest the same. You did. D'ye remember how you was when ye come back?

WEAVER: Yes! But with me it was a different matter. Then the thing was fresh, the feeling had not begun to die down.

TOM: It hain't never died down, Dick, an' don't think hit has. Ye can cover a thing like this ovah but ye can't kill hit.

WEAVER: You may feel that way but my hate is dead.

TOM (*slowly*): Then—then ye're leavin' us now?

WEAVER (*with a gesture of despair*): God! But I wish I could.

TOM (*triumphantly*): Thar! I knew ye wouldn't!

WEAVER: Don't be too sure. Don't push me to my limit. It's too late for me to begin again but I give you fair warning: Leave my boy alone. He shan't be driven into it.

TOM: Did we drive you into hit? Seems to me like you come 'cause ye wanted to.

WEAVER: You can say that now with some show of truth. A man will do queer things when his family is doing them, too. Well, no matter about that, maybe I did it of my own accord, maybe not.

TOM: We didn't push ye none.

WEAVER: Dick has got to be freed from all this. It will be your quarrel and my quarrel, if you must have it, but not his.

TOM: Ye ain't goin' to stop hit that way?

WEAVER: I give you my word not to— (*ironically*) not to desert the cause if we're to live on in hate and bitterness—but you've got to leave the boy alone! Never mention it to him again. When he comes back here to practice I want him to do it with clean hands. I had hoped we could come to some agreement today. If we can't—well, I've told you what I'll do.

TOM: Hit ain't enough!

WEAVER (*bitterly*): It's not enough! I've given up about everything I ever valued but it's not enough. What else have I, Tom, that you want to take from me? My boy? You know my terms. I'll stick but you can't have him.

TOM: You ain't doin' right puttin' these notions in Dick's head. That's what's wrong with Sam. Dick's been talkin' to him. Dick's his eyeballs enyway an' he'll listen to him quicker than he will to me. I tell ye I ain't goin' to have hit! I'll have Sam do my way if I have to skin him with a cowhide. (*Sam and Richard enter hurriedly.*)

SAM: It's startin' to pour down rain.

WEAVER: By the way, Tom, are you having any more trouble with that bank?

TOM: Yeah! I have nothin' but trouble with hit. (*Glancing*

out the window.) I hope hit don't rain steady. I meant to work on hit today, but I didn't have time.

WEAVER: Oh, I reckon it'll hold till morning.

(*It is getting dark. Mag brings in a smoky lamp and places it on the table.*)

MAG: Rainin', Tom.

TOM: Yeah!

WEAVER (*to Richard*): Well son, you picked a bad night to travel, didn't you?

RICHARD: One suits me as well as another, Pa.

WEAVER: Yes. It doesn't matter so much now. When I went off to school there were no trains up here. You can remember that far back, can't you, Tom?

TOM: I reckon I can. I helped lay the fust mile o' track in these mountains. That was while you was gone, Dick.

WEAVER: I had to walk over the mountains to Morganton. That was as far as the trains come. I started out early in the morning, son, with my pack on my back. (*Smiling.*) Almost everything I had was in that pack and God knows that wasn't much. It was a fine day too and I didn't mind the distance. Along toward sunset I came to Morganton. It was just a village but I'd never seen such a great place before. What a thrill it gave me![2] Oh—to be young like that again! And I enjoyed my youth so much.[3] I envy you, son.

SAM (*who has been listening intently*): Hit must be a great large place by now, Uncle Dick.

WEAVER (*smiling*): London or Morganton, Sammy?

SAM: Morganton.

WEAVER: Almost ten thousand people, Sammy.

SAM (*very quietly and almost as if speaking to himself*): I'd like to go thar. I'm goin' thar some day.

RICHARD (*very sophisticated*): Pshaw! It's nothing but a little village. You ought to see Philadelphia.

WEAVER: Dick will miss the thrill that you would get, Sammy. I've taken him away with me on my trips before.

---

2. Four lines deleted by the author.
3. One line deleted by the author (including allusion to London).

TOM: Well, he ain't goin' nowhar till he larns some sense an' gits some notions out'n his head.

WEAVER: We'll have to be going, Tom. This rain looks steady and Dick has some things to do before he's ready to go.

MAG (*protesting*): Ye'll git soakin' wet, Dick.

WEAVER: Oh no. The top's upon the buggy. Come on, son. Tell the folks good-bye. We must be going.

RICHARD: Good-bye, Uncle Tom. (*Shakes hands with him.*) Good-bye, Aunt Mag. (*She kisses him, to his great disgust.*) Good-bye, Sam. (*Doesn't take his hand. Stands rather awkwardly making talk.*) You—you'll take good care of Bob, won't you?

SAM (*miserably*): Can I hunt with him?

RICHARD: If you want to. (*Sam is overcome with emotion and begins to blubber, wiping his eyes with a grimy fist.*)

MAG: Say thank you to yore cousin Dick, Sammy. (*The only answer is another convulsive heave from Sam.*) I do declare the pore feller's cryin'.

SAM (*wiping at his eyes*): Aw—you!

RICHARD (*embarrassed*): Aw! I wouldn't be such a big baby!

SAM: Ye goin' to be gone long, Dick?

RICHARD: A good while, I reckon, Sam. But I'm coming back as soon as I'm a doctor and help Pa with his practice.

WEAVER: Spoken like a man, Dick.

RICHARD: I'll—I'll write to you, Sam.

SAM: All right.

TOM: Ah! What's the use o' writin' him? He cain't read. (*Sam looks angrily at his father.*)

WEAVER (*kindly*): That's all right, Sammy. You bring your letters to me and I'll read them to you.

RICHARD (*helplessly*): Well—good-bye! (*Starts to go hastily. Sam blubbers again. Richard looks pleadingly at his father.*) Pa!

WEAVER (*patting Sam on the back*): Here, here, Sammy. Brace up and play the man. Dick's not going away forever, you know.

SAM: We been good friens, ain't we, Dick?

RICHARD: Sure, we have. Well—good-bye. (*Doesn't move.*)

SAM (*to his father*): Thar! I tol' ye we'd been good friens.

MAG (*to Tom*): What ye been doin' to that boy? Have ye been pokin' fun at him agin?

TOM: Ah—he's a fool.

(*Weaver has been observing both his son and Sam intently. He now speaks winningly to Sam.*)

WEAVER: Sammy, d'ye ever think of going away from up here?

SAM: Whur d'ye mean, Uncle Dick?

WEAVER (*with a large gesture*): Oh—out yonder.

SAM: Away from up heah! (*He nods dumbly.*)

TOM: He's got some such notion, I reckon. All boys his age git hit. I had hit myself when I was young.

WEAVER: Like to get out and see things, eh? (*Nudges the boy with a chuckle. Sam grins delightedly.*)

SAM: I'd like to go to Morganton.

WEAVER: Got a mind for schooling, Sammy?

SAM: I'd like t' git some lurnin'. I don't know nothin'.

WEAVER: How'd you like to go away now, Sammy?

SAM: (*staring at him with slow fascination*): I'd—I'd like hit all right.

(*Weaver looks inquiringly at Tom.*)

WEAVER: Well, Tom? What do you think about it?

TOM (*puzzled*): What d'ye mean?

MAG (*with a snap*): He means what about Sam's goin' away and gittin' some schoolin'.

TOM (*violently*): No. I hain't got no money to go throwin' away on his schoolin'.

WEAVER (*patiently*): Yes. I know, Tom. I am ready to pay the bills myself. I'm not a rich man, but I can afford it. The boys have been together so long. I hate to see them parted now.

TOM: He couldn't go off with Dick. He don't know nothin'. He ain't never had no schoolin'. How could he start now?

MAG: Sam's as smart as the next one if he's got the chanct.

TOM: To heah you go on about him he might be King Solyman.

WEAVER: Of course Dick's a great deal farther advanced than Sam. But Dick has a tough road to go. I would send Sam to a good preparatory school for a few years and with hard work he might get ready for college. You'd study hard, wouldn't you, son?

SAM: Ye— Yes, sir.

WEAVER: Well, what do you say, Tom?

(*Tom feels trapped and looks with angry suspicion at his brother.*)

TOM: Ye ain't doin' this fer nothin', Dick. I know what ye're tryin' to do. Ye ain't got no right to go puttin' these notions in my boy's head. Ye're tryin' to git him away from me, that's what ye're tryin' to do!

WEAVER (*becoming frank, direct, brutal*): I can give your boy an education, new friends, a new outlook on life. What can you give him?

MAG: Nothin'!

TOM (*furiously*): You keep quiet, Mag. Don't ye come puttin' yore trap in now! (*Bitterly.*) I knowed ye would take sides agin me.

MAG: Ye ain't goin' to keep him from goin' Tom Weaver. Hit's his chanct an' he's goin' to have hit.

SAM: Paw, le'me go! Please!

WEAVER: Is there any good reason why you should keep him here, Tom?

TOM: I don't see no good in his goin' off. I never had no schoolin'.

MAG: An' look at ye now!

TOM: What's good enough fer me is good enough fer my boy, I reckon.

WEAVER: That's a very selfish attitude, Tom. You'd surely not keep him here because you never had the chance to go away.

MAG: No, an' he's not goin' to. Sam's dreamed about goin' away an' now that he's got the chance he ain't goin' to be cheated out of hit.

TOM: Ah! Ye're all agin me. Who's to do his work on the

farm? Will you tell me that? He's big enough to do a man's work now an' I cain't spare him.

SAM: I'll come back an' help ye, paw.

TOM: Yes ye will!

MAG: If ye cain't git along without'n his work, I'll do hit myself.

TOM: You?

MAG: Yes, me! I done harder work than farm work in my life an' I reckon I can do hit now. But Sam's goin'.

TOM (*weakly*): Well, I dunno—

(*Mag comes forward now, a gaunt but splendid Fury.*)

MAG: Yes, ye do, too. God! D'ye want to see him do like you had to do? D'ye want to see him slavin' his life away heah because he don't know nothin' else? Well, ye ain't goin' to keep him, now. He's got his chanct an' he's goin'.

(*Tom turns moodily away and walks to the window. In the silence that ensues the rain that comes beating against the house may be heard. There begins another sound, the sliding of sand and gravel down the slope. This quickly increases in amount and fury until it rises above the sound of the rain. Reese bursts breathlessly into the room.*)

REESE: She's comin' down, paw. Looks like the hull bank might cave in.

TOM: Go git the team an' haul a load of logs up heah. (*Reese goes out.*) You, Sam, come on with me. That damned hill!

(*The thud of heavy pieces of earth dropping off the bank may be heard.*)

God! Will we never stop that thing?

MAG (*soothingly*): Ye're goin' with yo're Uncle Dick, Sam.

TOM: He ain't goin' nowhere now. I was a fool to give in like I done. D'ye think I'll let him go runnin' off when I've got to put up with that?

MAG: Ye're goin' with yore Uncle Dick, Sammy. Don't ye pay no 'tenshun to yore paw.

TOM: By God, Mag. I could kill ye. I've put up with all yore goin's on I can. (*To Sam.*) Hair ye comin' with me or not?

WEAVER: He's her boy, too, Tom.

TOM (*beaten*): Oh—let him go ef he wants to.

SAM (*quietly*): I'll go on out with paw. He's right. I can't go.

MAG: Sammy!

(*He goes out blindly into the rain. Tom follows quickly. The noise of the sliding dirt increases in volume. Mag sits looking stonily ahead.*)

WEAVER (*gently*): I'm sorry, Mag, but perhaps he's right. The boy decided for himself. It would have been a great responsibility. I hardly knew whether I could have shouldered it with a clear conscience. Knowledge is sometimes a fearful, and awful thing. (*Musingly.*) To take this boy away from his people.

MAG: O God, Dick! Why didn't ye?

WEAVER: As much lost as gained perhaps. (*Shaking his head.*) I don't know, I don't know. Yet there's something fine about that boy.

MAG (*in dry tones*): My boy's as smart as the next one if he had the chanct.

(*Reese is heard cracking his whip and shouting to his team outside. Tom's voice may be heard commanding him to come in closer. There is a confused mingling of voices. Weaver with his boy's hand in his own turns to the door.*)

WEAVER: And now, son, we will go.

CURTAIN

ACT III

Weaver's living room has not changed greatly with the years, save in some imperceptible details. It is sundown of a day in early summer. The beams of the setting sun filter with misty redness through smoky storm clouds at the horizon's edge. There has been *a cloud-burst the night before; it has rained fitfully throughout the day. Now, the earth steams herself, the upper parts of the mountains are cloaked in thick, grey mists.*

At intervals there comes from the distance the hoarse blasts of a train whistle, which appears neither to advance nor recede. Much nearer at hand are sounds of human activity; there is heard occasionally the sound of a banjo being picked, accompanied by the heavy thump of boots and uneven drunken voices.

There are rapid footsteps along the road that runs before the house. A short, quick rapping on the door follows. Laura, grown to maturity and prettiness, passes by in the hall outside and opens the door.

LAURA: Is it you Sam? Why, what's the matter? Have you been running? You are out of breath.

(*Sam Weaver, now a lean, browned, not unattractive appearing young mountaineer of four and twenty, enters. His heavy, cowhide boots are mud-caked. He shows signs of fatigue and sits down, without speaking for a moment, in order to get his breath. Finally:—*)

SAM: Whar's Dick?

LAURA: What's the matter? Is anything wrong?

SAM: Listen: D'ye hear 'em goin' on down thar?

(*They are silent and the shouts and cries of the drunken men are heard.*)

LAURA: Where is that coming from—Gudger's store?

SAM: Yeah. They're all thar. This is the fust o' the month, ye know, an' those as works fer the lumber people got their pay. They started this mornin'. They're right smart lickered up now. I'm feared they're huntin' trouble, Laura. An' paw's riled the way they been actin'. Some one shot at Reese, ye know, a month back.

LAURA: Richard went to Bald Pate this morning.

SAM: He picked a nice wet day. Them rains last night fixed us, I reckon. Our cawn's gone away. An' that hill behind the house, the one paw's had so much trouble with, may slide down any time now.

LAURA: Is Uncle Tom at home?

SAM: No. I don't know whar he got to. He went off the fust thing this mornin'. When d'ye reckon Dick'll be back?

LAURA: He ought to be here now.

SAM: I hope he don't go by the sto' fer nothin'.

LAURA: Sam! What do you mean? Is he in any danger?

SAM: Mebbe. I don't know. It depends on how they feel. an' they're all thar, waitin'.

LAURA: You mean the Gudgers? (*He nods.*) But surely they have nothing against Dick. He was always friendly to them.

SAM: He's a Weaver, ain't he?

LAURA: But you don't know how he feels, Sam. He won't have anything to do with it. He says it's not his quarrel and he'll take no part in it.

SAM: Mebbe. What'd he come home fer, Laura?

LAURA: Well, why shouldn't he? It's his home, isn't it? Besides, pa's not as young as he once was and he needs Dick to help him.

SAM: Catch me comin' back to this God-forsaken place if I had his chance.

LAURA: He wants to help the people. He says they're his people and he couldn't leave them.

SAM (*with savage bitterness*): Help 'em? Lord, don't he know no better than that? I tell ye, nothin' can't help these people. They're as sorry, muleheaded an' low-lived critters as I ever seed. That's what they air, though I be one of 'em, an' shouldn't say it.

LAURA: Sam! You mustn't talk like that of your own people.

SAM (*with increasing bitterness*): My own people. What've they ever done fer me? Heah I am, twenty-four year old, an' I can't even read, much less write my own name. That's what they've done fer me. They've kep' me heah an' worked me like a dawg. An' I was a feller that might've made somethin' outa myself. I wanted larnin', Laura. I allus hankard to git hit. Now I'm no good fer nothin' but to wuk a pore, run down, measly farm an' tote a gun when they say the word. Good Gawd, I sometime wonder what I'm livin' fer.

LAURA: You poor boy! Yes I know what it's been. But, Sam, we must hope—

SAM: Hope? I've given up hopin', Laura. That ain't no way out fer me. Supposin' I did leave? Whar could I go? What could I do? Me that cain't even write his own name. I'd be a laughin'-stock. But with Dick hit's different. He kin git along anywhar now. Why in Gawd's name don't he? It's a murderin', bloody business heah an' he ain't cut out fer it.

LAURA: No, Sam. I know he's not. But he's determined to stay.

SAM: Ef I was him I'd pack up and git out right now, today. I wouldn't stay a minute longer.

LAURA: But he's home less than a week, Sam. Surely you wouldn't drive him off now.

SAM: I'm tellin' ye, Laura: He'd bettah go an' go now. I know what's what. He ain't goin' to make no headway heah an' he may git taken in hissif.

(*Footsteps are heard outside and Richard enters dressed in rough corduroys and serviceable walking shoes. He deposits his knapsack and cap on the table in the hall and enters the room with quick steps, and no signs of fatigue.*)

LAURA: Dick! Didn't you get soaking wet?

RICHARD: Oh, no. I was above the rains before they started. Hello, Sam. What brings you to town this time of the week?

SAM: I had a little chore to do, Dick. Ye don't look a mite petered out. Did ye go the hull way to the top o' Bald Pate?

RICHARD: Oh, yes. No, I don't feel tired at all. Great view from the top, Sam. It was like fairyland. Couldn't look below at all. Mist and fog all around. Just like you were in another world. I've a mind to go back every time it rains. That was a rain last night, wasn't it? There were washouts all along the way. At places the banks have slid down over the trails and covered them.

(*The train whistle blows several times.*)

LAURA: I wonder what can be the matter down there. That train has been blowing all afternoon. It should've been here at three o'clock.

SAM: I reckon there won't be no trains today. They've a slide on the track down the mountain an' they cain't git through.

RICHARD (*with a laugh*): Well, that's adventure for you, isn't it? You see, you don't have to hunt for it. It comes and finds you. We're just like people cast up on a desert isle—until the trains get through, at least.

SAM (*soberly*): Hit's Gawd-forsaken enough without them. I didn't know how I'd git along ef they didn't come.

RICHARD: Go on, Sam. You never rode on a train in your life. You'd get along just as well if there weren't any.

SAM: No, Dick. You don't know what hit means to me. When the train goes by our twenty-acre field every day I stop my ploughin' an' go to the fence an' watch hit till hit's gone. Hit's a down grade thar an' the train goes real slow. I could run along an' keep up with hit fer a spell ef I wanted to. Many's the time I've stood that feelin' jest like I was gettin' ready to jump offen a high place. I could climb that fence an' jump on an' be gone in a minute but somehow—

RICHARD: Somehow, things aren't done that way, are they? People don't tear themselves up by the roots in a minute, do they? No, I found that out, Sam, when I was away. I had to come back because I was planted here. Something seemed to tug and pull—and, well, you see, here I am. Now, here's little Laura—only she's not little any more—and I doubt if you could get her to leave.

LAURA: You'd better not give me the chance. I might fool you.

RICHARD: Yes, you would! You wouldn't be gone a week until you'd be wanting to see pine and balsam and look at blue hills again.

LAURA: You don't think I could leave?

RICHARD (*gravely*): You leave but you come back. I know that, Laura. They hem you in and hold you and never let you go.

LAURA (*with a shiver*): Oh, Dick. Please don't talk like that. You're enough to scare a body to death when you talk of them that way. It's like—it's like they were alive.

RICHARD: Who can say they aren't?

LAURA: Perhaps you've seen them move?

SAM (*quietly*): I have.

RICHARD: Sam knows it too.

(*They are all silent for a moment. Richard aroused himself with a start.*)

Well! It's getting late, isn't it? Has pa come in yet?

LAURA: No, Dick. He went to Beaverdam today. The roads are bad, I guess.

RICHARD: Terrible.

SAM: Well, I'll be goin'. Hit's gittin' late (*Awkwardly.*) Dick, I was goin' to say to you— (*He pauses, unable to continue.*)

RICHARD: Well?

SAM (*quietly after a pause*): Dick. I wouldn't go near the sto' ef I was you.

(*Richard regards him sharply for a moment.*)

RICHARD (*laughing*): Why, of course I will, if I want to. What's to keep me from it?

SAM: Thar may be trouble.

RICHARD (*slowly*): Oh, there may be trouble? (*Quickly.*) Well, what if there is? What have I to worry about? I've harmed no one.

SAM: Your name's Weaver, ain't it?

RICHARD: See here: they can't make me do anything I don't want to do. That's flat.

SAM: All right; but keep away from the sto' or they may do something to you you don't want 'em to do. The hull pack of Gudgers is down thar drinkin' an' goin' on, an' hit ain't safe fer you to be around 'em.

RICHARD (*quietly*): All right, Sam. I'll keep away. Take care of yourself. Don't get into any trouble.

SAM: Good-bye, Laura. 'Bye, Dick. (*He goes.*)

RICHARD: Sam's a nice, decent fellow. He's far above the average in intelligence. It seems a shame he's been kept down as he has. Uncle Tom's a regular old tyrant. I always have thought he's treated that boy badly because he saw something finer in him than he had in himself.

LAURA: Uncle Tom's stubborn and he's getting old, Dick, like pa.

RICHARD: I never could understand the hold he seems to have

over pa. I don't see why pa stands it from the old ignoramus!

LAURA: Dick! He's your uncle!

RICHARD: I don't care who he is. He's an ignorant old man and he's no right to try to force people into his narrow and bigoted way of thinking.

LAURA: But don't you understand, Dick, that Uncle Tom is no different from the rest of the people here? If anything he's more intelligent.

RICHARD: Then God help them!

LAURA (slyly): I thought you were going to do that.

RICHARD: I am. That is, I hope to.

LAURA: Then, don't you think you'd better show a little more sympathy and understanding toward them?

RICHARD: I am sympathetic. And I understand.

LAURA: If you put them down as narrow and bigoted—well, it's true, I know, but you can't blame them for it.

RICHARD: Yes, I know. The poor devils don't know there's a world going on outside these hills. They're shut in and crushed down from the cradle to the grave. If they try to leave, the mountains call them back. When they try to squeeze a living out of the ground the mountains give them a half living, killing them by inches.

LAURA (bluntly): Dick, why did you come back?

RICHARD (startled): That's a funny thing to say. Aren't you glad to see me?

LAURA (impatiently): Oh, you know how glad I am. But you know what you have to face here. Pa did his best but it was no use. I think Will Gudger's father tried to stop it but he couldn't.

RICHARD: The mob wins, eh? The Uncle Toms are in the majority.

LAURA: You know how we wanted you back but there have been times, Dick, when I hoped, I almost prayed you wouldn't come. I know what you want to do here. But, Dick, it seems so hopeless. They're so primitive, so terribly ignorant and so bitter.

RICHARD: Yes, I know that. But I tell you I had to come back. I couldn't have stayed away.

LAURA: You *wanted* to come back?

RICHARD: Oh, it wasn't a question of "wanting," it was a question of "had to." Laura, you never went around with pa on his visits as I did when I was a boy. You'd better be glad. God! what things I saw!

LAURA: I can guess.

RICHARD: I tell you that was a picture that was burnt into me—here. (*He taps his breast.*) It's never left me. During all those years I was away I was never really away. I had only to close my eyes and it would all come back to me. It was a picture that haunted and hurt.

LAURA: I know it's not pretty. There's not much romance to the life they lead, although the books all say there is, don't they?

RICHARD: If you should read a thousand books which told you of bare-foot girls with golden hair, you would know it's a lie, that they are raw, thin, ugly, and that their hands are big and rough from hard work. When you read a romance, think of its conclusion; they are married at eighteen, at twenty-five they are breeding droves, at thirty they are broken and old. Those are the facts; that is the truth. That is something most of us hate to face. And that was my picture. Once you see it, you will not forget it.

LAURA: I know. There was Tom Bryce's wife—

RICHARD: There's a case. Where is she now?

LAURA: She's dead.

RICHARD: Poor woman! What a life she led! What a story these hills could tell if they wanted to. They could tell of people eating, sleeping, dying in one room, fouled with the smell of dirty babies. They could tell of worn out women lying-in such places, giving birth to one child after another, while the dirty, unkempt little devils swarm around on the floor.

LAURA: Yet I love to read the books which paint it differently.

RICHARD: So do we all, perhaps. But the mountains are absolute realists. See what they do with their materials.

(*There are sounds of wheels on the road outside.*)

LAURA: There's pa, now.

RICHARD: I suppose he's done in.

LAURA: The poor man is kept going from morn to night. He is getting old fast, Dick. Had you noticed?

RICHARD: Yes. He can't stand the gaff any more. The pace is telling on him.

(*Weaver, trenched and worn by heavy years, enters with tired steps. He throws his hat and satchel wearily upon the hall table and tramps slowly into the room. We see his hair has become very grey: his mouth is molded in hard stubborn lines, and his eyes are paunched and dull, with tiny woven wrinkles at the sides. He brightens at once at sight of his children and his greeting is cheerful.*)

RICHARD: Good evening, pa.

LAURA (*affectionately*): You're tired out, pa. Sit down here.

(*He seats himself. She moves around him arranging a cushion beneath his head and making him comfortable.*)

WEAVER: Did you have a good day, son?

RICHARD: It was pretty wet going.

WEAVER: Oh, of course. It did rain. (*Holding Laura's hand.*) How's my little girl? (*Quietly and with great tenderness.*) Isn't she pretty, Dick?

RICHARD: Yes, pa.

WEAVER: She's her mother over again. (*He sighs.*) Ah, Lord honey—it's many a year since I was young, but I forget that when I look at you.

LAURA (*laughing uncertainly*): Listen to him! He talks as if he's an old man.

WEAVER: I am, honey, or I soon will be.

LAURA: Don't be silly. You're tired, pa. And I guess you're hungry. (*He nods with a smile.*) Have you been going all day?

WEAVER: Yes. Without a let-up.

LAURA: You poor man! You must be starved. I'll have supper now in a hurry. (*She starts to go.*)

WEAVER: Isn't it good to see her again, Dick?

RICHARD: It's good to see you both, pa.

WEAVER: You want to always stand by that girl, Dick. She's

the best friend we've got. She's never left me for a minute. And yet—I reckon I've got to lose her too. I can't keep her always. It's not right.

LAURA: Pa! You know I— (*She stops short and bites her lips.*)

WEAVER: You know the old saying, Dick: "*A son's a son till he gets him a wife, But a daughter's a daughter all the days of her life.*" How much truth is there in that?

LAURA (*going quickly*): I must hurry if we're to eat. (*She goes.*)

WEAVER: All right, my dear.

(*Richard regards his father in the silence that ensues first with professional curiosity, then with a look of affection and sympathy. Weaver's heavy body slumps limply in the chair, his eyes are fixed and stare before him, his manner is one of utter weariness.*)

RICHARD (*finally*): What have you done today?

WEAVER: I was out on Beaverdam the whole day long. There's a peculiar case out there. (*He laughs.*) It would be funny if it weren't so pathetic.

RICHARD: What is it?

WEAVER: There's a mountaineer out there with a sprained ankle. It seems the fellow saw an airplane fly at the county fair. He thought he could do the same. When he got home he took a pair of eagle's wings—given him by his father, he says—and somehow or other hitched them to his shoulders. Then, he climbed a tree and stepped off.

RICHARD: Is this a fact? (*Laughing.*) It's a wonder he didn't kill himself? (*After a moment.*) Poor ignorant devils.

WEAVER: And yet they're our own people, son. Yours and mine. We mustn't forget that.

RICHARD: Yes, I know. Only, we've gone pretty far beyond them.

WEAVER: Sometimes I wonder (*He closes his eyes wearily.*)

RICHARD: Pa, did you know you're in need of a rest?

WEAVER (*quickly*): Who said that?

RICHARD: I did.

WEAVER (*with a smile*): So it's come to this.

RICHARD: What's come?

WEAVER: Where is the boy—Dick Weaver? That was a man who spoke—and he's already sorry for his daddy.

RICHARD: No. It's not that, I hope. But you must slacken up, pa. You're all in. Remember I'm home to help you now. You've no need to kill yourself.

WEAVER (*with a smile*): And the first thing you want to take the reins right out of the old man's hand.

RICHARD: No. Not that. Merely to relieve you of part of your work: you do enough for two men.

WEAVER: The old horse hates to own he's not so spry as he was in the colt days. Sit down, Dick. There is something I want to say to you. (*Richard obeys.*) When you were a boy you learned something of conditions here. You saw ignorance and disease laying waste the people. You know it's not an attractive outlook. Yet, to a man inspired with a desire to serve, those conditions should set the mind on fire.

RICHARD: They do, pa.

WEAVER: I was just such a boy as you when I came back with your mother. I was young, strong as a mule, and full of fine schemes. Today I'm an old man, or soon will be, and most of those fine schemes were wrecked years ago. Son, it's a hard thing for a man to say of himself, because it's the last word, but as I look back over my life today I know I have not made it prevail. (*There is a long painful silence. Finally:—*)

RICHARD: Why?

WEAVER: There are many reasons but I suppose the chief one is my family. I couldn't get away from them. I became a partisan.

RICHARD: I'm sorry, pa. I've always been sorry about it. But I don't understand yet. I don't see why.

WEAVER: Your uncle is a primitive mountaineer like most of these people. I'm not. That's why you don't understand. But, Dick, your uncle and I were boys together; we grew up on the same little farm; we ate the same food, lived the same lives for eighteen years. That is a strong bond between men.

RICHARD: But you went away.

WEAVER: Yes—but I came back.

RICHARD: And what about me? It hits home if it is true.

WEAVER: You are free. That is the price I've paid, but it's worth it. They can't touch you. I've told them so. They say the old order changes. It never does. It dies. But you're not part of the old order. Praise God, son, you belong to the new order. And the track is clear for you. You can knock down the barriers, patch up the quarrels, be your own man and everyone's man. You can do the thing I wanted to do but couldn't.

RICHARD: It's a great chance. I will make the most of it. Fellows like Will Gudger and Sam and me know what we're about. Why should we bother ourselves because of a quarrel between two old men we never saw. The rest is simple.

WEAVER: Not simple son, but possible. Nothing is simple. I made that mistake. Most boys do, I guess. I thought life was simple and that a man could do either one thing or the other without hesitation. That's boy-like, you know. But life is painful and tangled up. It gives us an infinite number of choices and our decision is not always easy or right. Keep your eyes open and do the best you can. No man can do more. But don't expect to see the Angel and the Devil wrestling at every cross-road.

(*Laura's voice is heard, calling: "Supper's ready."*)

WEAVER (*Rising*): Let's not keep her waiting, Dick.

(*They go out into the hall. As they do there is a rapping on the door and Richard admits Will Gudger, now a florid, healthy looking young fellow of twenty-five.*)

RICHARD: Oh, hello, Will. Come in.

WILL: Hello, Dick. Good evening, doctor.

WEAVER: Good evening, Will. You haven't been here in some time, have you?

WILL: This has been a hard spring for me. All my trees are bearing for the first time.

WEAVER: That's a pretty place you have there, Will. I drove by the other day. You'll have a big crop this year.

WILL: It looks that way.

WEAVER: Is the place all yours?

WILL: Yes, sir. Papa gave me that land before I went off to school. He didn't think I could make it pay, though. It was no good for farming. But none of it is, sir. You can't raise vegetables on the side of a hill, but you can raise apples. They laughed at me when I came back and told them what I was going to do. Tom Bryce used to ask me how I was going to pick 'em—if I was going to stay at the foot of the hill and catch them as they rolled down. Well, he laughs on the other side of his mouth now. The spring rains came and washed his corn down the gulleys, but my trees are still there.

RICHARD (*laughing*): He changed his tune, did he?

WILL: Oh, no. He's too stubborn to do that, Dick. They all are. They'd starve to death rather than admit they're wrong.

WEAVER: I expect your father is pleased, though.

WILL: He doesn't say much, but I can see he is tickled to death.

WEAVER: How is your father?

WILL: Very well, thank you. (*A pause.*) He sends his regards.

WEAVER: Thank him for me—and give him mine. We are just going in to supper. Won't you join us?

WILL: No, thank you. I've just finished. I won't stay, then. I thought you would be through.

RICHARD: Did you want to see Laura?

WILL: I did, but I can come back later.

(*Laura's voice: "Is it you, Will? No, don't go. I'll be right out!"* *She comes up the hall, leaving her apron on the table as she passes.*)

WILL: I won't keep you, Laura. I'll be back later. I wanted to see you for a minute.

LAURA (*to Richard and Weaver*): It's on the table. Go ahead. I'll be back in a minute.

WEAVER: Then, if you won't join us, Will?—

(*Will nods negatively. Weaver and Richard go out. Will and Laura enter.*)

LAURA: What is it, Will?

WILL: See here, did you know a mob is gathering at the store?

LAURA: Yes, I heard. Are they making trouble?

WILL: No, but I'm afraid they're going to. And I hear Tom Weaver is driving all over the country getting his people together. Does your father know anything about it?

LAURA: No. He hasn't mentioned it.

WILL: Laura, if they start this thing again it's all up with you and me. I've waited for you long enough and I'm not going to be cheated out of you now.

LAURA: What are we to do?

WILL: They've got the track cleared; the train will be through at eight o'clock. Get some things together in a bag and meet me at the station.

LAURA: Will! What are you saying?

WILL (*doggedly*): I tell you it's the only way out. You've put me off and put me off, but you're not going to do it any more. I'll take you with me if I have to carry you away on my back.

LAURA: But what do you intend to do? Where are we going?

WILL: I'll take you to Stanton and marry you. Then we'll take a trip North. If there's trouble here they can howl and rave all they want to, but I shan't bring you back to it.

LAURA: But what of your beautiful orchard? Will, your heart's in that place. You couldn't give it up.

(*He appears to waver and for a moment thinks wistfully of his apple trees, but recalls himself and speaks with characteristic decision.*)

WILL: I can give it up if necessary. I'm not going to let them mess my life up, or yours either, Laura. If we can't be happy here I'll take you so far away they'll never reach us again.

LAURA: But, my dear, don't you see you'll be giving up everything?

WILL: Not if you come. And you've got to.

LAURA: Have you any plans?

WILL: I've money of my own saved up. And you needn't worry about getting along. I can make a living anywhere, Laura.

Would you like to go to California? I've a letter asking me to go out there and run a big orchard.

LAURA: Will, you're a good boy, and I love you. But I couldn't go. I couldn't. Do you know that every time I look at pa now-a-days I feel my heart will break. He looks so old and beaten. And, oh, Will, I've been so close to pa. If I should leave him now I don't know what would become of him.

WILL: Dick will be here to stay with him. (*After a pause.*) I guess he'll stay.

LAURA: And if he does—? Do you think he should, Will?

WILL: Laura, the wind will whistle through a hollow tree, but it blows the good trees down, sometimes. That happens in an orchard. But if it blows it blows, and you can't stop it. All your life you've been your father's girl. You've never left him. You've tended him, you've stood by him through thick and thin. No girl could do more. He has no right to expect more of you. He can't keep you always. It is not fair to you.

LAURA: It's no use. I can't go now. It's too wild an idea. I wouldn't let you do it. You'd be giving up too much you've worked for. People don't cut themselves away from things like that.

WILL: They do if they're brave enough. Is that the trouble? Are you so tied down here you're afraid to go?

LAURA: What are you saying? Those hills have been prison walls to me. Do you think it's easier to sit here at my knitting when the world is humming by outside?

WILL: You're three times seven. Aren't you free?

LAURA: That's a word, Will. We don't know what it means.

WILL: If you come with me we will know.

LAURA: But I've got to go with you. There's always an "if."

(*Steadily advancing a step closer.*)

WILL: Don't you want to go with me?

LAURA (*confused and overcome*): Will—I—Don't! Please.

(*He embraces her.*)

WILL: Laura, you've got to, you've got to. We can't wait forever like this and it's no good putting it off.

(*Richard enters.*)

RICHARD: Talking business, Will?

(*They part hurriedly.*)

  WILL (*after a moment*): You can help me if you want to, Dick.

RICHARD: Do you need help?

WILL: I've tried to persuade Laura to come with me—to go off now and marry me, but she won't listen. And I feel it's now or never.

RICHARD: Why are you in such a hurry?

(*There is a silence and from a distance comes sounds of the banjo being picked at the store with the untuneful accompaniment of drunken voices. Will makes an expressive gesture toward the sound.*)

Is that the reason? (*Will nods.*) Are you afraid of that? Surely we're not to be frightened off by the songs of drunken men?

WILL: You don't know. You can't tell.

RICHARD: Laura:—you like him, I know. Do you care enough for him to marry him? (*After a moment she nods.*) Well, what are you worried over, Will? You see how it is.

WILL: She says that, but she won't do it. Saying it does me a lot of good.

RICHARD (*to Laura*): What's the matter?

LAURA: Oh, I can't run off with him like this.

RICHARD: No, she can't, Will. Be reasonable. Do you want her to go off with hardly a word to pa? That would hurt him. I suppose you've said nothing to him, have you? These things can't be done on the spur of the moment. Why not set a reasonable time to get ready and then you can get married here where you've always lived, in your own home before all your people? Why should you sneak off as if you were doing something dishonest?

WILL (*bitterly*): A reasonable time! Yes, I know what that means: forever. Haven't I waited a reasonable time? Haven't I been patient? But always it's the same answer; wait. I'm sick of waiting. I didn't think it was in you to be so selfish, Dick.

RICHARD: Selfish? What have I done?

WILL: She won't leave because of you and your father. She doesn't want to leave you alone. Well, she's a right to her own life as much as any of you, and I don't think you've shown her much consideration.

LAURA: Will! Wait—

WILL (*making toward the door*): No, I won't wait. I've had enough of that.

RICHARD: Don't be foolish, Will. If you're in a hurry you can see my father tomorrow.

WILL: Why not right now?

RICHARD (*patiently*): As you like, Will. Only he's tired out tonight, for he's had a hard day. I think tomorrow would be better.

LAURA: Yes. Tomorrow is best, Will.

WILL (*starting to fling out*): Oh, well then:—tomorrow.

LAURA: You've not going away like that. You act mad as a wet hen.

WILL: Yes, and I've reason to.

LAURA: Come, now, let's see you smile.

WILL (*with a surly grin*): Oh, all right. Will that do? Good-night to you.

LAURA: Good-night, Will.

RICHARD: Will! Don't get the wrong idea. Laura's free to do as she chooses. Pa would be the last man in the world to stand in her way.

WILL: That's all right. I'm sorry. I was excited.

RICHARD: Then you can come back tomorrow.

WILL: All right. But no later. Tomorrow. (*He goes out.*)

RICHARD (*jestingly*): Now you're up against it. He's forced your hand.

LAURA (*rather helplessly*): What am I to do?

(*He takes her by the shoulders.*)

RICHARD: Do what you want to do. He's a good boy, Laura. There's some truth to what he said. You mustn't let pa or me stand in the way if you want him. It's hard to let you go. But we ought to be old enough to look after ourselves.

LAURA: Poor boy. It's been hard on him. And on me too. I've put it off so often. (*She hides her head in his shoulder.*)

RICHARD: There—old girl. Brace up, now, the worst is over.

LAURA: Those were long years you were away, Dick.

RICHARD: For me, too.

LAURA: We never thought of time before you went away. I never worried about getting older. Somehow it seemed we would be always together. Do you remember how you'd go off on long trips to the mountains and take me with you?

RICHARD: And pull you up behind me when you were tired and out of breath.

LAURA: And we'd sit on the top and look out—way out yonder—where it all gets blue and hazy and people can't look beyond it, and we'd wonder what it was all about and where that train way, way, out yonder was going. And you'd tell me the wild stories you thought up of the mountains, and how they were waiting and waiting until some day they would get people, like giants or fairies in old stories.

RICHARD (*gravely*): They get a great many, Laura. Do you remember the old stories of the magic circles fairies could put around people? And they couldn't ever get out.

LAURA: Those were lovely days. To be able to think things like that! People would never grow old if they always thought like that, for it would always be strange and wonderful. (*Wistfully.*) Could we bring them back again?

RICHARD: Why not?

LAURA (*with decision*): Of course we couldn't. We've other things to think of now.

(*There is a rapping at the door. Weaver passes by and admits his brother Tom. Tom has aged heavily. He is gaunt and bent; his hair and beard are shaggy and unkempt; his eyes are burning like a madman's.*)

TOM (*sharply*): I want to see you, Dick.

WEAVER (*cheerfully*): Well, here I am.

LAURA (*slightly annoyed by his brusqueness*): Hello, Uncle Tom. We're here, you know.

TOM (*curtly*): Hello, (*to Weaver.*) I want to see you alone.

WEAVER: All right. Come in. (*To Laura and Richard.*) Your uncle wants to see me alone. (*They start to go.*)

TOM (*in low tones nodding toward Richard*): Tell him to stay.

WEAVER: No. Tell me first. What has happened? (*Laura and Richard go out.*)

TOM (*trembling in suppressed rage and emotion*): Well, hit's come.

WEAVER: What is it? You're like a wild man!

TOM (*breathing rapidly, unable to control himself*): Oh, we'll have hit out now. I've seen all the boys an' they're comin' in.

WEAVER (*sharply*): Are you crazy? Why have you done that?

TOM: They're drinkin', an' goin' on, an' talkin' big down thar. Listen!

(*Again in the silence the cries and noises of the drunken men may be heard. Now and then, also, there is a shrill whoop.*)

They're sayin' thar ain't one of them as ain't good as any three of we'uns.

WEAVER: Are you going to listen to those drunk dogs?

TOM (*in rage and fury*): I tell ye I've had all I can stand. I ain't goin' to put up with hit no longer. They shot at my Reese a month back an' I ain't goin' to put up with it.

WEAVER: How do you know *they* shot at him?

TOM: Who else would've done hit?

WEAVER: You're making a big mistake forcing things this way. You have no right to stir up trouble like this.

TOM: Hit wan't me as started hit.

WEAVER: It will all blow over if you leave them alone. Why can't you?

TOM: I ain't goin' to take nothin' offen them. Call Dick in heah. I want to see him.

WEAVER: What do you want with him?

TOM: I reckon he'll want to be thar with us.

WEAVER: He'll want nothing of the sort.

TOM: He's yore own boy, ain't he? He'll want to be along with ye.

WEAVER: With me?

TOM: Yeah, with you.

WEAVER: Do you expect me to go with you?

TOM: I don't expect nothin'. I know ye'll come. You ain't goin' to turn agin yore own folks, Dick. Ye ain't goin' to leave us now atter stayin' by us all these years. Nor little Dick neither.

WEAVER: He's not little any more. He's a grown man and can do for himself. You leave him alone.

TOM: He ain't goin' to let his daddy go out by hisse'f. Not if I know a Weaver when I see one. We're a family as sticks together. I'll say that much.

WEAVER (*with an open threat in voice and manner*): I told you to leave him alone.

TOM (*stubbornly*): He's one of us an' you can't take him away.

WEAVER: He's not one of you and never will be. By God, I saw to that. You wanted me and you got me. But that's all you'll get.

TOM: Hit's his folks jist like hit's yourn. I don't see no difference.

WEAVER: I grew up with you and lived with you in my young days, that's the difference.

TOM: Ye ain't goin' to back out like this, Dick. We've stood by you an' yourn; now you got to do the right thing by yore folks. I'll let the boy be ef ye want hit that way, tho' he ain't got much spunk ef he lets you go by yourself, but you got to stick by us. You gave yore word. Ye ain't goin' to go back on it.

WEAVER: I told you if you were ever in danger I would stand by you. But I'll take no part in rows you pick yourself. I'm not out looking for trouble.

TOM: Thar was a time—

WEAVER (*curtly*): Don't throw that up to me now. I've my boy to look out for. When do you expect the men?

TOM: I told 'em to be heah at eight o'clock.

WEAVER: Here! At my house!

TOM: Yeah! That's all right, ain't it?

WEAVER: Well, they can turn right around and go home.

TOM: No, sir. They've double-dar'd weuns to show our face an' we ain't goin' to take it.

WEAVER: You're a crowd of children. Send them home when they come. This is the way these things start.

(*The door without is opened unceremoniously and Mag, wearing shawl and bonnet, comes in.*)

Good evening, Mag.

TOM (*startled*): What air ye doin' heah?

MAG: A fine one ye air to be stirrin' up trouble this way. An' yore own boy in town today alone with that drunken crowd.

TOM (*quickly*): Whar is Sam? Ef they've ha'med him—!

MAG: Aw, he's all right, but no thanks to you. I met him on the road an' made him go home.

TOM: I want him heah.

MAG: No you don't. You leave him be. Thar ain't no need fer trouble an' I ain't goin' to have him mixed up in no such 'goin's-on.

WEAVER: You're right, Mag. You've done a very foolish thing, Tom. The thing you must do now is to send the men home when they get here.

TOM (*muttering*): I don't know as I can. They're right smart lickered up themself.

WEAVER: You're a fine leader if you can't control them!

TOM: They're hard to manage when they git goin'. (*Roughly to Mag.*) You ain't got no business heah! You ought to be home tendin' to yore chores.

MAG: I come in to find my boy. Ef you tended to yore chores as well as I do ye wouldn't have no time to go aroun' huntin' up trouble.

TOM: That's my affair, I reckon.

MAG: The Lord knows, Tom Weaver, you have trouble enough of yore own without huntin' it from other folks. (*Appealing to Weaver.*) He ain't been at home the hull day an' all his young cawn was beat right into the ground by the rain last night. That's the way he tends to things.

TOM: I wanted to git away from the damn place. I feel like

I never want to see hit agin. Hit's nothin' but a trouble an' a grief to me. When the rains come all the water on Double-Top runs down into my back yard an' drowns my crops. The damn mountain causes half my trouble. That hill behind me is apt to slide down on me any time now. It's been creepin' an' slidin' down, slow an' easy, a few foot a year.

WEAVER: Can't you stop it?

TOM: How air ye goin' to stop a mountain by drivin' a few sticks o' wood in the ground? Me an' my boys worked all Spring doin' that but hit don't do no good. No: hit'll git me some day.

WEAVER: It's too bad you built your home in such a place.

MAG: That's what I allus told him.

TOM: What else could I do? I had to git some pertection agin the weather.

(*There is a rapping at the door, slow and hesitant. Richard opens it and admits Roberts, a sallow, middle-aged mountaineer, at present agitated by a severe emotional strain, but determined to give the impression of calmness.*)

ROBERTS: Is Doc Weaver in?

RICHARD: Yes, come in. A man to see you, pa.

(*They enter. Tom surveys the man sharply and suspiciously. Roberts returns the gaze with evident discomfort.*)

WEAVER: You want to see me? What is it?

ROBERTS: Doc, my little gal's been took down with a fever an' a cough. At times it looks like she can't git her breath. I come to ask ye to go with me out to my place.

WEAVER: Where do you live?

ROBERTS: Out on Beaverdam. I have a team outside.

TOM: Ain't yore name Roberts?

ROBERTS (*a trifle defiantly*): Clem Roberts my name.

TOM: This feller's a cousin o' the Gudgers.

RICHARD: It doesn't matter who he is. One of us ought to go with him.

(*The man looks gratefully at Richard.*)

WEAVER: Of course I'll go. Here, Roberts, take this prescription down to Joe Winston and have him fill it. You'll have to go to his house, the store's closed. Hurry, now, and get back as soon as you can. I'll be ready. (*Roberts goes quickly.*)

TOM (*protesting*): You ain't goin' out thar with that feller, air ye?

WEAVER: Why not? I'm a doctor, Tom, and personal likes or dislikes has nothing to do with the matter. I can't refuse my services to a man because I don't like his people.

TOM: Jest the same we got to stick together. Right now most of all. I don't like to see ye goin' out thar with any o' that gang. Hit don't look right. Folks'll talk.

WEAVER (*hitting his brother on the back*): Pshaw, Tom, don't make a mountain of a mole-hill. Think of the man's little girl. You can't let a child suffer, you know.

TOM (*grumbling*): Well, do as ye like, then.

WEAVER: That's right. I can depend on you to send the men home without any trouble, can't I?

TOM: I'll see what I can do.

WEAVER: There's no excuse for trouble, you know. We don't want it said of us we hunted it. (*To Richard.*) Son, you'll have to entertain your uncle while I'm gone. Tell Laura not to wait up. It'll be midnight before I'm back.

RICHARD: All right, pa. If you want me to go along—?

WEAVER: No, no. Stay where you are. I won't need you. I'll be in my office putting some things together. Call me when Roberts returns (*He goes out.*)

(*The attitude of Tom and Richard, left together, shows marked restraint. Richard is cold; at first his manner conveys something akin to actual distaste. Tom is the first to break the silence. He turns his head, spits tobacco juice accurately toward the hearth, and surveys his nephew curiously.*)

TOM: Well, Dick, I ain't seen as much of you as I'd have liked to since ye got back.

RICHARD: No?

TOM: You ain't been out to see us.

RICHARD: I've just got settled. I hope all you folks have been well.

TOM: Tolable. The ole gal's been complainin'.

RICHARD: You mean Aunt Mag—?

TOM: Yeah. The ole woman. But she's allus ailin' an' complainin' of one thing or t'other.

RICHARD: What's the matter with her?

TOM: Oh, hit's been her back heah lately. But ef hit ain't her back hit's somethin' else.

RICHARD: Maybe she's overworked herself.

TOM: Wuk. What's a woman know 'bout hit? Hit's me as wuks. Course, they piddle aroun' the house a leetle.

RICHARD: Sew and cook a little, perhaps.

TOM: Yeah.

RICHARD: Wash and iron, some I suppose. Take care of the house and look after the children but, after all, they don't do much work.

TOM: Well, no. Not what you'd call work.

RICHARD: What do you call work, Uncle Tom?

TOM: Oh, hoein' an' grubbin' in the fields under a bilin' sun, an' gittin' things to grow atter the rains wash away what you've planted. That's work.

RICHARD: Yes. I agree with you. That's work. But the other's work, too.

TOM: I reckon the ole gal has had a hard time. We ain't as young as we once was, Dick.

RICHARD: Go on! You talk as if you were an old man.

TOM (*earnestly*): I am, Dick. I am.

RICHARD: You're not over forty-five and Aunt Mag's not forty yet, is she?

TOM: She's goin' on forty-one. But we been through a lot, Dick. Oh, Lord, son, that's what tells on a man. A man's a fool as will try to farm a piece o' mountain land. All my life I've done it. An' I ain't good fer nothin' else. Ef I had my time over again—well, you'd better be glad you don't have to. Yore paw's done a lot fer you, Dick.

RICHARD: Yes. I know he has, Uncle Tom.

TOM: I reckon you'd do a lot fer yore paw, Dick.

RICHARD: Anything in the world. (*After a moment.*) Anything in my power.

TOM: Yore paw was jest such a boy as you air when he come back. He allus did have a lot of get-up-an'-go to him. When he said he'd do a thing he'd do it. He said he was goin' off an' study to be a doctor an' he went. Sometimes I wonder if he did right then.

RICHARD (*impatiently*): Of course he did. What would he have amounted to if he'd stayed here all his life?

TOM: He'd have been a good fer nothin' like me, ye mean? (*Richard doesn't answer.*) Well, I know hit makes a difference. Yore paw an' I never have been the same since he went away. But I'll say hit to his credit he's stood by us. He wan't ashamed of his family.

RICHARD: That would be foolish. My father would have been rich and famous if he had stayed in the city. He had the ability. But he came back and gave his life to these people here. I wonder if you know what that means. That was a fine thing to do because he knew it was not for the moment but for the rest of his life.

TOM: Is that what you mean to do, Dick?

RICHARD: Yes. That is what I want to do.

TOM: Well, that's right. I allus thought ye'd come back like yore paw. I reckon weuns as is raised heah wouldn't feel right no other place.

RICHARD: There's that, too.

TOM: You said you'd do anything fer yore paw. Ef you knowed, now, that someone had it in fer him—

RICHARD (*quickly*): What do you mean?

TOM (*slowly and persuasively*): That thar was folks as didn't like yore paw.

RICHARD: Tell me what you're driving at. What do you know?

TOM: Folks as might even shoot at yore paw, in the dark, so that they'd find him in the mornin' with a hole in him.

RICHARD: That's not true. He's harmed no one. What could they have against him? (*He laughs uneasily.*) That's a joke!

TOM: He's raised you up to be a fine gentleman. Mebbe you're too good fer weuns. That's all right ef you want hit that way. I can see yore p'int. Mebbe we'll see some day if they can gentleman the Weaver blood out of ye. I don't know 'bout that. Ef that time comes look'e in the closet thar. (*He points.*) I've kep' something thar fer ye.

(*Richard starts toward the closet. Weaver returns. He notices Richard's perturbation and looks sharply at Tom.*)

WEAVER: Has Roberts come back?

RICHARD: Not yet, pa. (*There are footsteps on the porch.*) There he is now.

(*There is a knocking at the door.*)

WEAVER: No, it's someone else. See who it is, Dick.

(*Richard opens the door. A mountaineer enters. The man scarcely controls his high excitement. His voice trembles slightly.*)

THE MAN: Is Tom Weaver heah?

RICHARD: Yes. Come in.

TOM: What it is, Dave? (*Starting forward.*) What's the matter?

DAVE: Tom! They've done fer yore boy, Sam. (*Dead silence.*)

TOM: What?

WEAVER: Where is he? } *Together.*

RICHARD: But he was here not long ago.

DAVE: We found him up the road in his wagon. The team was still movin' on home.

TOM (*overcome by rage and grief, begins to talk to himself*): I knowed hit! I knowed hit! My own boy! Shot like a dawg— He wan't given a chance— I seen this comin' on. Now, by God, we'll see. We'll see ef they can do weuns that way.

WEAVER: Try to control yourself, Tom, until you learn the whole truth of this.

(*Mag and Laura enter.*)

MAG: What is it, Tom? (*She notices the strained and sympathetic faces of the others.*) Tom, what is it?

TOM (*with something like tenderness*): Go home, Mag, an' meet yore boy when he gits thar. They've done fer him.

MAG (*in low, hardly audible tones*): Sam? D'ye mean my Sam?

(*He nods.*)

TOM (*to Dave*): Aiz the boys heah?

DAVE: They're comin' up the road.

TOM: They know?

DAVE: Yeah, Tom. They're ready now.

(*Along the road at a distance is heard the sound of many footsteps, approaching on the run.*)

TOM (*to Weaver*): Get ready, Dick. I'll meet 'em outside when they git back. We'll wait on you.

(*Richard starts and regards both men with astonishment. Weaver, after a moment, gives a brief nod of affirmation.*)

WEAVER: All right, Tom.

TOM (*to Richard*): Son, ef yore paw—

WEAVER (*seizing Tom by the shoulder*): Don't forget, Tom! (*Tom looks toward the closet, then at Richard.*)

TOM: Come on, Dave. (*They go out.*)

LAURA: Aunt Mag, please sit down. (*She leads her to a chair.*)

MAG: Whar's Tom?

LAURA: Why, didn't you see him? He just went out. (*To Richard.*) Poor thing. She doesn't know what's happening.

MAG (*dully*): Yeah. I know, honey. You'd better hope you'll never know as well. They'll try to settle hit now by shootin' an' killin' each other. But that don't do no good. That don't bring my boy back.

RICHARD (*gently*): No, Aunt Mag. You know more than they do.

MAG: My boy's gone. Well, why ain't that best? He never fitted in with the rest, no way. Now they can't drive an' pester him no more. Now they can't kill him by long days o' work—him that was cut out fer something better. They killed him quick, when he was young. He won't never have to go through what I been through. Now, God bless him.

LAURA: Uncle Tom—

MAG: Tom, what does he keer? Does he think o' me? I've knowed him come thirty year an' now most likely he'll go out thar an' git killed. But does he keer? Does he think o' me?

WEAVER (*to Laura*): Take her to your room, Laura, and let her rest. (*Laura leads her out.*)

RICHARD: It is terrible. He was here not long ago talking of going away. Must boys like that be sacrificed to the mob? Will they go on shooting and killing until there are no more left to shoot and kill? Why can't we stop it?

(*There are cries and shouts and the stamping of heavy boots from afar at the store. Above these sounds, in monotonous rise and fall, comes the notes of the banjo. And now there are added other sounds—oaths and angry muttered voices on the road without and the rapid thud of many feet upon the earth. There are cries of "We're here," "we're ready," "let's go get them," "Tom Weaver, are you there?" etc.*)

RICHARD (*looking out*): They are there, in a mob. (*He goes to the door.*)

LAURA (*shrinking back*): Dick, stay here.

SEVERAL VOICES OUTSIDE: Doc. Weaver! Come on out!

TOM: We're waitin' on ye, Dick.

(*Richard starts and moves hastily.*)

WEAVER (*quietly*): It's me they're calling, son.

(*There is dead silence. Weaver moves toward the door.*)

RICHARD (*hoarsely*): Pa. In God's name! You're not going out there!

WEAVER (*dumbly*): I've got to, son.

RICHARD (*seizing him desperately*): You can't. I won't let you.

WEAVER (*releasing himself*): I've got to.

RICHARD (*falling back in horror*): A man like you—with that mob.

(*Impatient shouts without.*)

WEAVER: Yes. A man like me—with that mob.

RICHARD (*desperately*): But you said—

WEAVER: Son, we're not much different from that mountaineer who thought he was a bird. We get wings but we can't fly with them.

RICHARD: Have you forgotten your profession entirely? Are you going with them and desert that sick child?

WEAVER: These are my people—my people.

(*Angry cries from the men outside. Robert's voice is heard, pleading desperately: "Leave me be. I ain't never ha'med you. Leave me be now. I got to see Doc Weaver. I got a sick baby at home."*)

(*Weaver hastens to the window and commands sharply:—*)

Leave that man alone. Come on in, Roberts. They won't bother you. (*Roberts enters.*)

ROBERTS: I'm ready, Doc. We'd better not lose no more time.

WEAVER: Roberts. I'm sorry—

RICHARD (*averting his head*): Pa! Don't.

WEAVER: I'm sorry, Roberts, but I can't go with you now.

ROBERTS: Doc! You said you would. What am I goin' to do now? The ole woman's nigh crazy 'bout the gal. Ef I come back without you I don't know what she'll do. Aw, doc, you don't mean hit.

WEAVER: I'm sorry. Something has happened that makes it impossible.

(*Roberts turns appealingly to Richard.*)

RICHARD: Yes, Roberts.

WEAVER: My son will go with you. You had better go now, Dick.

RICHARD: Wait for me outside, Roberts. There are some things I must get here.

ROBERTS (*anxiously*): Ye won't be long.

RICHARD: No, Roberts. (*Roberts goes out.*)

WEAVER: You will find everything you need in my satchel. It's on the table there. (*Laura enters.*)

LAURA: You are going with Roberts, Dick?

RICHARD: Yes. (*To Weaver.*) Are you determined to do this thing?

WEAVER: I have no choice.

RICHARD: You have no choice? Are you to be moved about by a crowd of ignorant men who don't know what they're fighting for? Only hate, hate—that's all they know. You have had discipline and education. What does it mean if you let yourself be forced like this?

WEAVER: Son, I know what I'm saying. I have no choice.

LAURA: Dick! You mustn't blame pa. He's saved you from this.

RICHARD: Haven't I seen enough murder eating its way through this family? Hasn't there been enough of killing over the quarrel of two old men I never saw? Didn't my own mother die because—

WEAVER (*hoarsely*): Stop, Dick!

RICHARD (*controlling himself*): I'm sorry. I didn't mean to say that. (*He mutters to himself.*) I won't go. I won't go, I tell you.

WEAVER: No! You don't have to, son. Go with the man, Roberts.

(*Cries outside. Weaver starts to go.*)

RICHARD (*desperately*): Pa!

(*Weaver, startled by his tone, looks at him intently. He passes his hand before his vision as a man dazed.*)

WEAVER: Son! What is the matter?

RICHARD: I can't let you go! (*Angry cries outside.*)

WEAVER (*slowly*): I didn't expect this.

(*He goes quickly. There are wild cries now from both sides. The music at the store has ceased, savage taunts are hurled back and forth between the waiting clans. Richard stands apparently incapable of thought or action.*)

LAURA: The man is waiting for you, Dick.

RICHARD (*mechanically*): The man—who?

LAURA: The man Roberts, who has the sick child.

RICHARD: Oh, yes. The man with the sick child.

LAURA: Are you going with him, Dick?

RICHARD (*turning and looking steadily at her*): So pa went with them, after all. With that damned, dirty mob.

LAURA: He's an old man, Dick. He's out there alone.

(*A crescendo of angry yells outside.*)

RICHARD: The mob. The dirty, ignorant mob.

LAURA: He's an old man, Dick. I've watched him grow old.

(*She cries out what is strong within her.*)

You can't let him go alone!

(*There is a silence.*)

RICHARD: No. I can't.

(*Roberts comes in quietly and stands in the entrance.*)

ROBERTS: I'm waitin'.

RICHARD: Go home, Roberts.

ROBERTS: You ain't comin'?

RICHARD: No. Not now.

ROBERTS: You gave your word.

RICHARD: I'm sorry. I can't go with you now.

ROBERTS (*in a voice trembling with passion and grief*): All right. All right, young Weaver. But I'll never fergit this. Not as long as I live. You ain't goin' to do me this way. No man ain't. I've never ha'med you nor yourn, but ef anything happens to my leetle gal, I'll—

RICHARD: That talk does you no good. Get out, Roberts.

ROBERTS (*in a grief-choked voice*): You ain't goin' to do me like this. No man ain't I'll get even—You wait—

(*He rushes out.*)

LAURA: You are going with them?

RICHARD: Yes. I am going with them.

LAURA (*in a low tone*): I'm sorry, Dick.

RICHARD: What must be, must be.

LAURA: It is your family.

RICHARD: It's those accursed mountains. They never let go.

(*A train whistle blows nearby.*)[4]

4. Stage direction added in pencil.

LAURA (*dry-eyed, but choking*): It's too bad, Dick.

RICHARD: I was a prophet in the wilderness too soon. The mountains aren't ready to receive prophets.

(*Mag enters; her face now as expressionless and stony as that of a statue. Richard jeers himself cruelly.*)

If the mountains won't come to Mahomet Weaver, why, then, Mahomet Weaver must go to the mountains.

(*The mob outside begins to move along the road toward the store. Those in the van break into a run. Shrill cries.*)

LAURA (*running to the window*): They are going to the store. (*Falling back with a sob.*) Oh!—There's pa among them. (*As if to herself.*) Will said he would come tomorrow.

RICHARD (*averting his head*): Tomorrow!

MAG: I reckon ye'd better go along, Dick. I ain't never seen no way out.

(*Richard goes rapidly to the closet, takes out his rifle and fills his pockets with cartridges. He snaps the barrel open and looks along its polished rim.*)

RICHARD (*preoccupied*): It's been kept in good shape, I see.

MAG: Yeah. Tom kep' hit fer ye.

RICHARD (*snapping the barrel shut*): O, God! They are drawing me in.

(*He goes to the window and, for the moment forgetting all else but himself and the hills before him, speaks in steady, conversational tones.*)

You can't see them. There's a fog around them. They plot and plan with a fog around them.

LAURA: The fog is lifting, Dick.

RICHARD: It is over. They've just played one of their little jokes. And they think it's very funny. See. Bald Pate is grinning. He thinks it's very funny. By God, they are laughing at me. It's now the proper time to laugh.

LAURA (*in terror*): Dick! Dick! Are you crazy? You mustn't talk like that. (*A shot is heard.*) Dick! Go now. They're waiting out there!

RICHARD: That's how they get you. They can wait the longest.

LAURA: You are going?

RICHARD (*at the door*): Yes. You always go when they want you.

(*He goes. His running footsteps may be heard along the road for some time. The two women stare at each other. Finally:—*)

LAURA: Why has this got to be, Mag?

MAG: Lord, child, don't ask me now! I don't know, I reckon thar ain't no way o' findin' out.

(*With a shrill, swiftly dying whistle, the train sweeps through and is gone.*)

(*Dully.*) The train got through.

LAURA: The world went by.

(*There are shots outside. The whistle blows faintly down the mountain.*)

CURTAIN